NATURE
THROUGH THE
EYES OF JOB

NEAL JONES

TRILOGY
A WHOLLY OWNED SUBSIDIARY OF **TBN**
PROFESSIONAL PUBLISHING MEETS POWERFUL PROMOTION

Nature through the Eyes of Job

Trilogy Christian Publishers
A Wholly Owned Subsidiary of Trinity Broadcasting Network
2442 Michelle Drive, Tustin, CA 92780

Copyright © 2024 by Neal Jones

Unless otherwise noted, scripture quotations are taken from the New American Standard Bible® (NASB), Copyright © 1960, 1962, 1963, 1968, 1971, 1972, 1973, 1975, 1977, 1995 by The Lockman Foundation. Used by permission. www.Lockman.org.

Scripture quotations marked CSB are taken from the Christian Standard Bible®, Copyright © 2017 by Holman Bible Publishers. Used by permission. Christian Standard Bible, and CSB®, are federally registered trademarks of Holman Bible Publishers.

Scripture quotations marked DARBY are taken from the Darby Bible.

Scripture quotations marked ESV are taken from the ESV® Bible (The Holy Bible, English Standard Version®), copyright © 2001 by Crossway Bibles, a publishing ministry of Good News Publishers. Used by permission. All rights reserved.

Scripture quotations marked KJV taken from The Holy Bible, King James Version. Cambridge Edition: 1769.

Scripture quotations marked NIV are taken from the Holy Bible, New International Version®, NIV®. Copyright © 1973, 1978, 1984, 2011 by Biblica, Inc.™ Used by permission of Zondervan. All rights reserved worldwide. *www.zondervan.com*. The "NIV" and "New International Version" are trademarks registered in the United States Patent and Trademark Office by Biblica, Inc.™

Scripture quotations marked NLT are taken from the Holy Bible, New Living Translation, copyright © 1996, 2004, 2015 by Tyndale House Foundation. Used by permission of Tyndale House Publishers, Inc., Carol Stream, Illinois 60188. All rights reserved.

All rights reserved, including the right to reproduce this book or portions thereof in any form whatsoever. For information, address Trilogy Christian Publishing Rights Department, 2442 Michelle Drive, Tustin, CA 92780.

Trilogy Christian Publishing/ TBN and colophon are trademarks of Trinity Broadcasting Network.

For information about special discounts for bulk purchases, please contact Trilogy Christian Publishing.

Trilogy Disclaimer: The views and content expressed in this book are those of the author and may not necessarily reflect the views and doctrine of Trilogy Christian Publishing or the Trinity Broadcasting Network.

10 9 8 7 6 5 4 3 2 1
Library of Congress Cataloging-in-Publication Data is available.

ISBN 979-8-89333-229-2
ISBN (ebook) 979-8-89333-230-8

DEDICATION

At first I didn't think I would do a dedication. But I thought about it further and the Lord put a thought in my head.

I would like to dedicate this book to all those people who have suffered loss or undergone trials that have just brought them to the very edge.

God allowed everything to be taken from Job except for one thing — his LIFE!

> *So the Lord said to Satan, "Behold, he is in your power, only spare his life."*
>
> —Job 2:6

FOREWORD

It was my pleasure to have served with Neal for many years at our small church in New York. He was one of my elders. It was my privilege to marry him and his dear wife, Becky. What a joy to see their family grow up in the Lord. Our congregation thoroughly enjoyed the Adult Sunday School classes he taught. He will always be one of my most treasured co-workers for the Kingdom.

> *Out of the ground the LORD God formed every beast of the field and every bird of the sky, and brought them to the man to see what he would call them; and whatever the man called a living creature, that was its name. The man gave names to all the cattle, and to the birds of the sky, and to every beast of the field...*
> — Genesis 2:19-20

What a chore that must have been. Not only did Adam have no internet, he had no zoological textbooks. It was a simple matter of carefully observing all these animals one by one and then comparing and contrasting them. How many different kinds of cattle could there have been? How many kinds of birds or beasts? Did he come up with some kind of system? Perhaps he used the idea of *Kingdom - Phylum - Class - Order - Family - Genus - Species*. We don't know. He did, however, come up with all their names.

In the end, Adam must have become quite the zoologist. Keep in mind that each animal was made by the same Creator. It must have been interesting for God to look upon Adam and see how he accomplished this task. Years later, God used some of the animals Adam named to teach Job about what kind of God He was and is. More recently, God did the same thing for my brother in Christ, Neal Jones.

Systematically, Neal went through the book of Job to see what could be learned about God through the animals He had created. Neal wanted to look at "nature through the eyes of Job." As he takes the reader through observations about the raptor, the hawk, the Verreaux's eagle, or even the great behemoth, Neal accurately blends science with the Holy Scriptures. He reiterates again and again that God has a plan, and we can see God's character in His creation. We can see His love, justice, patience, gentleness, and integrity.

Have a wonderful trip, dear reader, as you take a look at *Nature Through the Eyes of Job*. Sit back and allow God to reveal Himself to you.

— Roger Hofmann,
February 2024

PREFACE

I majored in wildlife and the environment at the University of New Hampshire. In several of my classes I was taught not only an evolutionary point of view but that Christianity was one of the main reasons for pollution and the exploitation of the environment! They stated that in Genesis, Christians believe they were given "dominion" over nature. Therefore, Christians felt that they had the "God given right" to take and exploit nature as they wanted. This was taught in contrast to other "faiths," "religions" or "cultures" that respected and revered nature.

In my sophomore year, I came to accept Jesus Christ as my personal Lord and Savior. I was discipled and active in Campus Crusade for Christ (now called CRU). It was here that I came to understand no amount of education or knowledge could change a person's heart. What truly changed a person was coming to God through Jesus Christ. Then, allowing the Holy Spirit and an understanding of the Scriptures to make us a new creation, transform us. If I really wanted to have a positive impact upon the environment I needed to point men back to God, through the person of Jesus Christ. Only then would knowledge of the environment have a true change in one's life.

I was also personally challenged when someone told me I couldn't hunt or fish as a "Christian." They proceeded to tell me how "your God" says, "Thou shall not kill."

As a new believer this had me wonder: what was a healthy Christian (Biblical) view of nature? Let me tell you, God was eager to teach me! Creation and God's Word exploded into a display beyond words. The next thing to hit me was the Book of Job.

In Job 1:8 and Job 2:3, God asks Satan, "Have you considered My servant Job? For there is no one like him on the earth, a blameless and upright man, fearing God and turning away from evil."

Here was the most blameless, upright man in all the earth (God's words — not mine).

In Job 38-41, God spoke to Job, but never answered his question. Instead, God reveals Himself to Job as Creator. What effect did this have on Job, the man of whom God Himself said there was no one else on earth like him?

In Job 42:1-6, Job states, "I have heard of You by the hearing of the ear; but now my eye sees you…"

Romans 1:20, "For since the creation of the world His invisible attributes, His eternal power and divine nature, have been clearly seen, being understood through what has been made, so that they are without excuse."

The man God said had "no one like him on earth" now understood God better than before! God tangibly revealed Himself to Job through a close look at His creation!

After graduating college, I spent several years studying and learning the Scriptures. Under the tutelage of several steadfast men of God, I studied theology, doctrine, biblical history, anything I could get my hands on to give me a better handle on the Word of God.

It is God's "general revelation" of Himself to all mankind. And, if you examine it closely, you see the distinct brush strokes of the Creator.

I want to see God "through Job's eyes," and I hope you can also.

PROLOGUE

I learned the prologue is mostly used in "fictional" books. Even though Job is not a fictional book, I felt compelled to write this in order to give the reader a little bit of a better understanding of who Job was and what exactly was going on in his story.

The author of the book of Job is unknown. Numerous suggestions have been given as to plausible authors. Most likely it would have been an eyewitness that could record the detailed and lengthy conversations found in the book. During Old Testament times, authors sometimes referred to themselves in the third person, so Job's authorship is a strong possibility.

Chronologically the Book of Job is considered by many to be the oldest or first Book of the Old Testament. The Book of Job is listed with the other "wisdom" books such as Proverbs. It is generally believed that Job himself lived during the time of the patriarchs. He lived in the land of Uz (which many scholars believe was located somewhere in northern Arabia).

Job was a very wealthy and respected man. He suffered the loss of his wealth, his family, and his health. This is all layered upon him in rapid succession at the hand of Satan with God's "apparent" consent. Job's supposed friends go to him to console him. Instead of comforting Job, they end up accusing Job of wrongdoing as the reason for all his misfortune and God's "judgement."

I find that many readers simply go from:

1. Job suffered loss
2. Job's defense against accusations
3. God speaks to Job as Creator
4. God restores Job twofold.

Most Biblical studies of Job are focused on the debate or discussion in chapters 3-37. This part of the account is very important and cannot be overlooked or taken lightly.

But I find most commentators just gloss over the "details" of God's discourse with Job. They simply say how God declared His greatness as Creator. If this is the main truth God was trying to get across, why did Job have such a drastic response? Job already knew God created everything!

I believe one should give a closer look at this "general revelation" with the same effort and depth given to the rest of the Book of Job.

TABLE OF CONTENTS

Dedication iii
Foreword v
Preface vii
Prologue xi

Chapter 1: Let Me Introduce Myself! (Job 38:1) 17
Chapter 2: Where Were You? (Job 38:4) 23
Chapter 3: A Firm Foundation (Job 38:4) 27
Chapter 4: I've Got a Plan! (Job 38:5, 6) 33
Chapter 5: "Just How Big Is Big?" *or*
    "It Ain't Gonna Happen!!" (Job 38:5) 37
Chapter 6: "My Friend" *or* "Let's Talk" 43
Chapter 7: "Let's Get Something Straight" *or*
    "Happy Day" (Job 38:6, 7) 49
Chapter 8: "Water, Water Everywhere..." (Job 38:8-11) . 55
Chapter 9: "Morning Has Broken..." (Job 38:12-15) . . . 61
Chapter 10: "Voyage to the Bottom of the Sea"
    (Job 38:16-18) 67
Chapter 11: "O Death, Where Is Thy Sting?"
    (Job 38:17, 18) 73
Chapter 12: "Where Do You Live?" (Job 38:19-21) 85
Chapter 13: Seeing Things as "Black or Light"
    (Job 38:19-21) 95
Chapter 14: "Can You Tell Me How to Get to...?" *or*
    "Good Day" (Job 38:19-21) 101

Chapter 15: "Stormy Weather" *or*
"There Will Be a Day" (Job 38:22-30) . . . 107

Chapter 16: "Only in the Dark Can You See the
Stars" *or* "Connecting the Dots"
(Job 38:31-33). 117

Chapter 17: "And Now, for the Local Forecast" *or*
"Can You Do This?" (Job 38:34-38). 125

Chapter 18: "Anything You Have Done, I Have Done
Better" (Job 38:39-41). 133

Chapter 19: "You've Got to Be Kiddin' Me!!" *or*
"Timing Is Everything!!" (Job 39:1-4) . . . 141

Chapter 20: "Who Let the Dogs (Donkeys) Out!!!"
(Job 39: 5-12). 149

Chapter 21: "As Strong as an Ox" *or*
"Do You Trust Me?" (Job 39:9-12) 157

Chapter 22: "That Just Doesn't Make Any Sense" *or*
"Batteries Not Included" *or*
"You Are Who I Say You Are"
(Job 39:13-18). 163

Chapter 23: "Remember the Source of Your Strength"
or "I'm Not Horsing Around"
(Job 39:9-25) 177

Chapter 24: "Free as a Bird" *or*
"Out of Your Hands" (Job 39: 26-30). . . . 185

Chapter 25: "That Says It All" *or*
"I've Said Too Much Already" *and*
"We're Not Finished Yet" (Job 40:2) 193

Chapter 26: "So You Think You're Qualified for
the Job" *or* "Let's Take a Good Look at
Things" (Job 40:8-14). 201

Chapter 27: "Behold" (Job 40: 15-24) 205
Chapter 28: "Can You... Will He... Who Can?" *or*
       "Your Worst Nightmare!" (Job 41:1-34). . . 213
Chapter 29: "Do You Realize Who I Am?" (Job 41:34) . 223
Chapter 30: "Get Real!" *or*
       "Open the Eyes of My Heart, Lord."
       (Job 42:1-6). 231
Chapter 31: "Why?" 241
Chapter 32: Not "Why?" but "Who?" 249
Chapter 33: "It's Not What You Know but Who You
       Know" *or* "It's Not WHAT You See but
       WHO You See!" (Job 42:5, 6). 257

Afterword 263

CHAPTER 1:
Let Me Introduce Myself!

There's nothing like a great introduction or entry. In the Bible we can find God "introducing Himself." These introductions can tell us something about God. They fill us with expectations and excite us about what we are going to hear or what is about to take place. Other times, we're glad we weren't there to witness His coming on the scene, because just reading about it terrifies us.

In the Book of Job, we have such an introduction.

> *Then the Lord answered Job out of the whirlwind and said...*
>
> —Job 38:1

Now in Job 31:35-37, we have Job's last recorded speech before seeing the Lord. Job cried out:

> *"Oh, that I had one to hear me! Here is my mark. Oh, that the Almighty would answer me, that my Prosecutor had written a book! Surely I would carry it on my shoulder, and bind it on me like a crown; I would declare to Him the number of my steps; like a prince I would approach Him."*

Well, here in Chapter 38, Job is about to have his request answered! The "prince" was about to have his day in court.

The word used here for "whirlwind" has also been translated "tempest." This was often a violent, noisy, and destructive storm. These storms often came out of the south. Elihu saw the storm forming and approaching and brought it to Job's attention as part of his discourse (Job 37). He tells Job to "listen" and mentions the "lightning," the "layer of thick clouds," the heat and winds out of the south. He describes the sky as a "molten mirror" and the darkness ("Now men do not see the light which is bright in the skies...").

A tornado usually moves from southwest to northeast. Their path of destruction can average four miles but has been known to reach up to 300 miles. The width of this path can be 400 yards or more. Tornadoes can travel at a speed of 25 to 40 mph, with wind speeds ranging from 65 to 200 mph. They typically originate from dark, heavy clouds with a swirling funnel-shaped pendant that extends to the ground. Preceding the storm, a heavy downpour with hail usually occurs. Tornadoes are generally characterized by a roaring, rushing sound like an airplane or trains speeding through a tunnel.

Scripture presents a "whirlwind" as showing the mighty power and judgement of "Yahweh."

> *The Lord is slow to anger and great in power, and the Lord will by no means leave the guilty unpunished. In a whirlwind and storm is His way and clouds are the dust beneath His feet.*
> — Nahum 1:3

> *The clouds poured out water; The skies gave forth a sound; Your arrows flashed here and there, the sound of Your thunder was in the whirlwind; The lightning lit up the world; The earth trembled and shook.*
> — Psalms 77:17-18

God appeared to Ezekiel in a whirlwind (Ezekiel 1:1-4). He also brought Elijah into heaven by a whirlwind (2 Kings 2:1,11).

The whirlwind is often associated with God's divine presence. It speaks to us of the powerful, unmanageable nature of God; like a tornado, He cannot be controlled or opposed.

God gives a little bit of a "twist" to His introduction when He *spoke* to Elijah in 1 Kings 19:11-13!

> So He said, "Go forth and stand on the mountain before the Lord."
>
> And behold, the Lord was passing by! And a great and strong wind was rending the mountain and breaking in pieces the rocks before the Lord; but the Lord was not in the wind. And after the wind an earthquake, but the Lord was not in the earthquake. After the earthquake a fire, but the Lord was not in the fire; and after the fire a sound of a gentle blowing. When Elijah heard it, he wrapped his face in his mantle and went out and stood in the entrance of the cave.
>
> And behold, a voice came to him and said, "What are you doing here, Elijah?"

God doesn't always stir up a storm when He wants to talk with us though! In Genesis 3:8, "Then the man and his wife heard the sound of the Lord God as He was walking in the garden in the cool of the day (a good rendering of this would read "evening breeze") and they hid from the Lord God among the trees of the garden."

But when our Lord returns, it will not go unnoticed!

> Our God comes and will not be silent; a fire devours before Him, and around Him a tempest rages. He summons the heavens above, and the earth, that He May judge His people…
>
> — Psalm 50:3-4

God uses nature to touch us, not only in our physical senses, but sometimes deeper and emotionally as well. So enjoy the cool evening breeze and keep an eye on the weather!!

CHAPTER 2:
Where Were You?

History never interested me when I was younger. It was just a list of dates and events. I never really understood how they affected my life. Then, as I got older, I looked back and saw that events in history were happening during my lifetime. I could see how certain events changed the way we did things, both for the good and the bad.

If we were lucky enough to talk to someone who "was there" we could hear the inside scoop on what really happened! Where were you when President Kennedy or Martin Luther King Jr. were shot? Where were you when a man walked on the moon? The list of "historical events" during my life just keeps adding up! Where were you on 9/11/01?

Science is also interested in "history": where and when did life and everything else begin? It's a valid question, and one that I hope we can take a serious look at "as time goes on."

Science is not "history." But "history" is used in some extent to see the "cause and effect" of certain events from the past.

When looking at past events, history and science have something in common. Both try and obtain information as close to the actual event as possible.

A recent example of this would be the airplane that crashed in the Mediterranean Sea, just off the coast of Egypt. We wanted to know why this happened. Was there a problem on the plane, or was it caused by something else? Questions sprang up everywhere. Both history and science would seek to find the answers. Both would want to talk to any «eyewitnesses," if they could find them. What did they hear? What did they see? The answer to these questions would help both scientists and historians get a more accurate picture of what took place.

In Job 31 we hear Job's final defense of his innocence. But he stepped over the fine line and began to question God's methods and wanted God to give answers as to "why bad things happen to good people." God turned the tables in Job 38:2-3 and asked Job about all this nonsense He's been listening to and then challenges Job to answer a few questions!!

In Job 38:4 we have one of the most important questions ever asked in the Bible. It's a question that we all need to examine and ask ourselves. The answer we come up with can eventually shake us or strengthen us: "Where were you when I laid the foundation of the earth..."

The first part of the question is easy, and our answer would be the same as Job's. "We weren't there! We weren't even around in the beginning!!" Wow! Even the simplest of scientists can tell you that!!!

It's the second point in the question that we often overlook and modern science sweeps under the rug. It's the second point of the question that Job understood, and it was now being brought to the forefront! It's a statement upon which the rest of God's questions would be hinged — "when I LAID the foundation of the earth." God not only put Himself there when it happened but made the bold assertion that HE DID IT!! He was the beginning, He is the "Creator God"!

This core truth is one of the key foundations of our faith. If He is not your Creator God, hopefully we can have you take a better look. (Romans 1:20 "For since the creation of the world, His invisible attributes, His eternal power and divine nature, have been clearly seen, being understood through what has been made, so that they are without excuse.")

If He is your Creator God, and you know our Lord Jesus Christ, hopefully your eyes can be opened to a deeper knowledge and appreciation of Him.

> *Raise your eyes on high And see who has created these stars, The One who brings out their multitude by number, He calls them all by name; Because of the greatness of His might and the strength of His power, Not one of them is missing.*
>
> — Isaiah 40:26

So, the next time you listen to someone expounding upon the "Big Bang," "Evolution," or "billions and billions of years," ask the same question that God asked Job, "Where were you when I laid the foundation of the earth?" Then talk to the ONE that was an "eyewitness" as to what took place.

CHAPTER 3:
A Firm Foundation

Did you ever just stop to think about the ground you're standing on? I mean, it's there every morning when you get out of bed. I am also personally aware of it after I get off an airplane, and thankful that my feet are back on "solid ground."

In Job 38:4, God makes a profound statement when He says, "Where were you when I laid the foundation of the earth?"

So, what kind of "foundation" was God talking about? For those that think God was talking about a "global foundation" and that somehow Job pictured a "flat earth on a pedestal," as the Egyptians and some other ancient cultures did, (the

Greeks declared that it was carried on the back of Atlas) you're forgetting Job's statement in 26:7: "He stretches out the north over empty space and hangs the earth on nothing." (This was a scientifically correct answer from a man that lived almost 2000 years before Christ.) God is referring to the ground Job was standing on. The earth's core!!

Whenever there is an earthquake, shock waves travel throughout the interior of the earth. But there is one area in which the waves act differently or fail to penetrate. That area is the earth's core, the very central part or "foundation" of the earth.

Until recently, seismologists assumed that the center of the earth was composed of molten iron. Scientists now believe that the core may be rocky. No one knows for certain. Our concept of the outer layers of the earth's crust has significantly changed in recent years; how much more so our ideas of the earth's interior?

Seismologists have found that the inner core is not completely uniform. Instead, they believe it contains large-scale structures. In addition to this, the properties of the inner core's surface vary from place to place. This variation can be across distances of less than a mile. Recent discoveries suggest that the solid inner core itself is composed of layers. These layers are separated by a transition zone. It is also believed that the core of the earth rotates at a faster speed than the rest of the earth. This is believed to help create and also affect the "magnetic fields" of the earth.

Science has shown the current solid inner core started solidifying out of a fully molten core *after* planetary formation. If true, this would mean that the Earth's solid inner core is not a primordial feature that was present during the planet's formation. This actually makes it a feature younger than the rest of the Earth.

Here is the fun part!! If we go back to Genesis 1:1-2, we see God creating the heavens and the earth (the planet). "In the beginning God created the heavens and the earth. The earth was formless and void, and darkness was over the surface of the deep, and the Spirit of God was moving over the surface of the waters."

It wasn't till the third day that God laid the foundation of the "earth"!!!

In Genesis 1:9-10: "And God said, Let the waters under the heaven be gathered together unto one place, and let the dry land appear: and it was so. And God called the dry land earth; and the gathering together of the waters He called the seas: and God saw that it was good." This would make the "foundation" appear younger than when the planet was formed!!

Foundations are a vital part of anything that's going to last. This is also true in all of nature. A good example from nature would be trees. Trees are nature's skyscrapers, and the better their roots are able to lock into the soil, the more stable they stand.

The giant sequoia in California named "General Sherman" is believed to be the largest tree on earth. This tree is an estimated 52,500+ cubic feet in volume (that's 410+ cords of wood to you wood burners!) and stands 274.9 feet tall, with a circumference at the ground of 102.6 feet. The first large branch is 130 feet above the base of the tree and has a diameter of 6.8 feet. A branch that fell from the tree in 1978 had a diameter greater than six feet and was at least 140 feet long. (This "branch" was larger than any tree in the US east of the Sierra Nevada and Cascades mountain ranges!!)

It is not uncommon to find the area covered by the tree's roots to be several times the size of the tree's height. The sequoias have a matting, shallow, and wide spreading root system. There is no taproot. The roots go 12 to 14 feet deep even at maturity. A mature sequoia's roots can occupy over an acre of earth and contain over 90,000 cubic feet of soil. That mass of matted roots and soil has to maintain the stability of a tree that is nearly 300 feet tall and weighs nearly two million pounds.

But what about our personal foundation? God speaks to us about it as well:

> *He is like a man which built a house, and dug deep, and laid the foundation on a rock: and when the flood arose, the storm beat vehemently upon that house, and could not shake it: for it was founded upon a rock.*
> — Luke 6:48

Generally, roots do not grow where the soil is too compact or there is not enough oxygen or moisture. Contrary to a common misconception, roots do not grow towards anything! Why do roots grow where they do? Roots grow where the resources of life are available!

> *Blessed is the one who does not walk with the wicked or stand in the way of sinners or sit in the company of mockers, but whose delight is in the law of the Lord, and who meditates on his law day and night.*

> *That person is like a tree planted by streams of water, which yields its fruit in season and whose leaf does not wither — whatever they do prospers.*
>
> — Psalm 1:1-3

In Job 38:4, God talked about laying the foundation of the earth. He wanted to bring Job back to the beginning. And it's here that He lays a foundation for Job (and us) to grow.

CHAPTER 4:
I've Got a Plan!

In Job 38:56 God once again asks Job a two tiered question: "Who determined its measurements — surely you know! Or who stretched the line upon it? On what were its bases sunk, or who laid its cornerstone?"

It's amazing how God wants us, in the midst of chaos, to take our eyes off the storm and look at Him, like Peter walking on the water. (Matthew 14:30 "But when he saw the wind, he was afraid, and beginning to sink he cried out, 'Lord, save me.'") Like a loving father telling his son, "Look at me, when I'm talking to you," God wants Job to refocus. He wants Job to not only listen to what is being said, but think about "who's saying it."

Many times in the OT to "measure" something communicated ownership. (As in Habakkuk 3:6, "He stood and measured the earth; he looked and shook the nations; then the eternal mountains were scattered; the everlasting hills sank low. His were the everlasting ways.") God wanted Job to focus on the fact that He's in control. And like the events in nature, the events going on in Job's life didn't just happen.

Are you an "inventor?" I'm not. But I am impressed by and thankful for those who are. Archimedes was a mathematician and inventor. He was born around 290 to 280 BC, in Syracuse, Sicily. Archimedes is credited with discovering the relationship between the surface and volume of a sphere and its circumscribing cylinder (basically he had discovered the number pi). He then formulated a "hydrostatic principle" based on that mathematical relationship called "Archimedes' principle." He invented the Archimedes screw (or hydraulic screw) that raised water from a lower to a higher level. Archimedes also invented the catapult, the lever, and the compound pulley. WOW! Where would we be without inventors and some of the modern inventions that we use on a regular basis? Who thinks of these things?!!!

Now, have you ever built anything from scratch? I've done mostly carpentry, spending some time after college as a cabinet maker. From there I was a "home missionary" serving as the maintenance supervisor for the mission. I found myself doing carpentry, plumbing, electrical, ground work and much more. No matter what I built, the first thing I needed was a "plan." This meant measurements, materials, and assembly.

With all this "building stuff," I really don't care to work on cars or trucks. So, I decided to take the "scientific method." I took a pile of metal and waited. I waited several years and slowly things started coming together. The heat from the sun, the movement of the wind, the water from the rain. First it was the nuts and bolts that formed, then the frame. It was amazing!!! Just the right size, just the right amount of material! At first it didn't fit together, but the pieces just bounced around some more. Several more years passed and PRESTO!! I had my first car. It even had the keys! All it took was a lot of "time" and things just came together.

Okay, okay! That wasn't a true story. But it puts the concept of creation without a Creator into perspective.

Try this: take a bolt, along with a washer and nut that fit it. Put the three items separately into a box. Now shake the box so that the washer goes onto the bolt and then the nut tightens onto the bolt.

First question: is this even possible? If you say yes, you are correct. But you probably also think you are going to win the lottery every time you play. (The last time I looked, chances on the Power-Ball was 1 in over 292 million.)

Now let's up the ante a little and put several bolts, washers, and nuts into the box. "More chances to win," right? Actually, you've just multiplied the difficulty of getting them together. How about if we go even further and put in several different size bolts with their proper washers and nuts. You've just exponentially increased the difficulty with each different nut and bolt combination. "Possible"? Yes! But how long would it take? The time would be beyond us and unable to be calculated. You would have to make an "educated guess" at best. (Yet this is exactly what "science" does with creation when it takes God out of the equation! We'll take a look at how "science" has come up with its timeline at a later date).

In order for the Big Bang and evolution to work, you need time — a LOT of it (you even have to violate a few natural laws along the way). Science had to create its own rules in order for their "theories" to work. (We'll also look at this later.)

If we can see the genius and understand the concept of inventing something new, if we can see the need for a design and plan for what we build, why then, when it comes to the ENORMOUS complexity of creation do we throw logic and reasoning out the window?

> *For even though they knew God, they did not honor Him as God or give thanks, but they became futile in their speculations, and their foolish heart was darkened. Professing to be wise, they became fools, and exchanged the glory of the incorruptible God for an image in the form of corruptible man and of birds and four-footed animals and crawling creatures.*
> — Romans 1:21-23

There is a plan and a purpose behind everything God does. He wanted Job and us to focus on the vastness of creation and ALL it contains. Then ask yourself the questions, "Who thought up ALL this?" and "Who really owns it?"

CHAPTER 5:

"Just How Big Is Big?" *or* "It Ain't Gonna Happen!!"

Last time we saw God having Job look at the "Who" in the creation picture. But God also made another point: creation has its limits and He's the One who set them.

Job 38:5 says "Who set its measurements? Since you know. Or who stretched the line on it?"

In these two questions, God makes the assertion that there is a set size and limit to creation. It literally means to "prescribe its boundaries." God says He designed and built it!

So, "Just how big does science say the universe is?" Here are some answers:

> *"But the size of the universe depends on a number of things, including its shape and expansion. Just how big is the universe? The truth is, scientists can't put a number on it."*
>
> — Nola Taylor Redd, space.com

> *But there's got to be a limit, right? It's not like the universe is infinite, right? Right? Well, probably not. While it is very, very, very large, the universe is not likely infinitely big.*
>
> — Paul Sutter, astrophysicist,
> June 8, 2016, space.com

Almost all scientists say there is a limit and boundaries to the universe. The "Big Bang Theory" holds that the universe started at a point in time and location and is expanding out like a giant cosmic balloon. In fact, the process is called "inflation."

> *This view of the universe fits with the current popular idea that the universe began with a vast expansion of size. This idea describes a kind of undirected energy present in the vacuum of space. This undirected energy is called scalar fields, and 'somehow' got channeled into a process called 'inflation.' By conservative estimates,*

> *the universe expanded so much during this period that something the size of an atom inflated to the size of a galaxy.*
>
> — Brent Tully, NOVA

Over and over again scientists say, "Honestly, we don't know." But, like good scientists, they don't and can't settle for that answer. So, they come up with "possible" answers.

When all is said and done, everyone pretty much agrees that the universe has its limits and what is beyond those limits, science says "we don't know."

So, how big is big? Recently (2006), the New Horizons spacecraft blasted off on a ten-year express flight to Pluto. (A manned flight to Pluto, at the maximum speed of the Apollo astronauts, would take about 17 years.) If the Sun-Pluto distance were represented by a one-foot ruler, the nearest star would be over a mile away. Real interstellar travel is limited by the speed of light (186,282 miles per second). Traveling at the speed of light, it would take an estimated 100,000 years for the full spiral of our galaxy to become visible. As for the earth — if the galaxy were represented as the size of North America, our entire solar system would fit in a coffee cup somewhere in Idaho. Human travel to the stars remains a dream.

Astronomers estimate that there are as many galaxies outside the Milky Way as there are stars in it. If true, that would mean there are more than 100 billion galaxies in the visible universe. Many of those galaxies hold more than 100 billion stars each. (According to Psalm 147:4, God calls them all by name.)

How big are the heavens and how is the foundation of the earth set? I can say with certainty that man will never know.

But you say, "Neal, with science and technology advancing so rapidly, how can you say that! There are things being done today that people never dreamed possible and said could never be done!"

Well, I can only make that statement because the One who created the heavens and the earth said so!

> *It is the Lord who provides the sun to light the day and the moon and stars to light the night, and who stirs the sea into roaring waves. His name is the Lord of Heaven's Armies, and this is what He says: I am as likely to reject my people Israel as I am to abolish the laws of nature! This is what the Lord says: Just as the heavens cannot be measured and foundations of the earth cannot be explored, so I will not consider casting them away for the evil they have done, I, the Lord have spoken!*
>
> — Jeremiah 31:35-37 NLT

God is true and faithful to His Word and His promises. If the heavens can be measured and the foundation of the earth explored, then it's possible for God to give up on His people. "It ain't gonna happen!!"

And, how big is big? I think Solomon put it "wisely" when he planned to build the Temple:

> *This must be a magnificent Temple because our God is greater than all other gods. But who can really build*

Him a worthy home? Not even the highest Heavens can contain Him! So who am I to consider building a Temple for Him, except as a place to burn sacrifices to Him?

— 2 Chronicles 2:5-6

Here in Job 38:5 God was telling Job: "Look around you, Job; I own it — I made it. I set its limits, and I'm bigger than you can imagine."

So we have to ask ourselves along with Job: "How big is my God?

CHAPTER 6:

"My Friend" *or* "Let's Talk"

And Job died, an old man, and full of days.

— Job 42:17

I want to take a quick, but important, break in our progress through Job's encounter with God.

The reason for this is, I want us to keep perspective on what exactly was happening. Remember, we are invited to "listen in" on this conversation.

We know that God is both COMPLETELY MERCIFUL and COMPLETELY JUST at the same time. God will punish sin, and the wages of sin is death (Romans 6:23). But God "disciplines" His children in order to restore them (Hebrews 12). Same God, same judge, different relationships, different results.

In the narrative of Job, we are "reading" the "verbal conversation" that God is having with Job. In a literary account of a verbal conversation, we often miss the facets such as "tone of voice," and more important, the "relationship."

Our relationship to the person we are communicating with goes a long way, both in how we put forth a message, and how a message is received.

- Are they a friend, family, boss, employee, stranger, etc.?
- How well do you know them, and how well do they know you?

Your relationship to the other parties in a conversation is going to have an impact on how you both express and respond to a message.

What I'm trying to say is this:

As we read this "verbal communication" between God and Job, we need to keep in mind who "they are" and "their relationship." This will open our minds and hearts to hopefully "hear" what is being said.

God and Job had a real relationship. We see this in the first two chapters of the book.

> *And the LORD said to Satan, "Have you considered my servant Job, that there is none like him on the*

earth, a blameless and upright man, who fears God and turns away from evil?"

— Job 1:8

And he (Job) said, "Naked I came from my mother's womb, and naked shall I return. The LORD gave, and the LORD has taken away; blessed be the name of the LORD." In all this Job did not sin or charge God with wrong.

— Job 1:21-22

And the LORD said to Satan, "Have you considered my servant Job, that there is none like him on the earth, a blameless and upright man, who fears God and turns away from evil? He still holds fast his integrity, although you incited me against him to destroy him without reason."

— Job 2:3

Then his wife said to him, "Do you still hold fast your integrity? Curse God and die."
But he said to her, "You speak as one of the foolish women would speak. Shall we receive good from God, and shall we not receive evil?" In all this Job did not sin with his lips.

— Job 2:9-10

We saw in Job 38:1-7 God presenting Himself to Job as the all-powerful, all-knowing, bigger than life Creator. But HOW God does this, and how Job is humbled, is also important.

God could have very easily come in and just hammered Job. But He didn't! Instead, what we see is God presenting Himself to Job as not only a God in control, but an understanding and caring Lord.

In Scripture, God sets forth how we are to deal with others. God does not expect more from us than He does of Himself. I could fill page after page with Scripture referencing the love of God. This would only illustrate what God is so desperately trying to have us (and Job) understand.

> *But God, being rich in mercy, because of His great love with which He loved us.*
> — Ephesians 2:4

> *Therefore I, the prisoner of the Lord, implore you to walk in a manner worthy of the calling with which you have been called, with all humility and gentleness, with patience, showing tolerance for one another in love, being diligent to preserve the unity of the Spirit in the bond of peace.*
> — Ephesians 4:1-3

Do you get the picture!!! God has not come to Job as a heavy-handed tyrant or disciplinarian. He didn't come to hammer Job for "screwing up." God Himself said He had "no reason" to bring these hardships upon Job!! Was God now going to punish Job for not understanding what was happening to him? Was God going to come in and just lay a big guilt trip on Job (as his friends did) for asking Him "Why?"!! Even as parents, we wouldn't do that to our children.

Personally, as a father (and many other fathers do this as well) I've looked at my boys and said, "You know better!" or "Let's think about this."

Instead, what we see in the next few questions are the words from a loving, caring Lord, a God that understood just what Job was feeling and why!

> *He still holds fast his integrity, although you incited*
> *me against him to destroy him without reason.*
>
> —Job 2:3

Job stepped over the line, but God stepped in to bring him back. God isn't telling Job anything that he didn't already know. But God was "refocusing" Job. Job was starting to wander off course in dealing with all the accusations of his "friends" (Job 38:2, "Who is this that darkens counsel by words without knowledge?")

God opened the eyes of Job into a better and closer understanding of the God he loved so much. God is reaffirming His relationship with Job. Remember in the final chapter of the book how differently He deals between Job and the others.

> *And it was so, that after the LORD had spoken*
> *these words unto Job, the LORD said to Eliphaz the*
> *Temanite, "My wrath is kindled against thee, and*
> *against thy two friends: for ye have not spoken of me*
> *the thing that is right, as my servant Job hath.*
>
> *"Therefore, take unto you now seven bullocks and*
> *seven rams, and go to my servant Job, and offer up for*
> *yourselves a burnt offering; and my servant Job shall*

pray for you: for him will I accept: lest I deal with you after your folly, in that ye have not spoken of me the thing which is right, like my servant Job."

So Eliphaz the Temanite and Bildad the Shuhite and Zophar the Naamathite went, and did according as the LORD commanded them: the LORD also accepted Job. And the LORD restored Job, when he prayed for his friends: also the LORD gave Job twice as much as he had before."

God never accused Job, but did require sacrifices from the others, and had Job pray for them. God then accepts the prayer of Job.

To think of God's conversation with Job as one of a Judge, rather than a Father, would be to fall into the same trap as the others.

In the following glimpses of nature, remember and think about God's "relationship" to Job (as well as His relationship to us). Then, let us try to catch His "tone of voice," as we once again "listen in" on God's conversation with Job.

CHAPTER 7:

"Let's Get Something Straight" *or* "Happy Day"

As we saw in Job 38:5, God once again expanded Job's thinking and directed him towards the WHO. We can't help but praise God as He points to Himself and pretty much says "Who can compare to Me!" With each question He's revealing more and more of Himself. He's getting bigger and Bigger and BIGGER. There is no end in sight!!!

In Job 38:6-7, God pointed out to Job something that he knew, but at the same time didn't understand.

God has already laid claim to the foundation of the earth (38:4). But every builder knows that you "have to put the foundation ON SOMETHING." God states that the earth was placed in a "specific spot." "On what were its bases sunk? Or who laid its cornerstone."

Both of these are building terms that Job would have been familiar with.

The first one would be similar to what a builder today would call a "footer." (Footings are an important part of foundation construction. Today they are typically made of concrete with rebar reinforcement that has been poured into an excavated trench. The purpose of footings is to support the foundation and prevent settling.

Placement of footings is crucial to provide the proper support for the foundation and ultimately the entire structure.

The second term is "cornerstone." The cornerstone or "foundation stone" concept is derived from the first stone set in the construction of a masonry foundation. It is vitally important since all other stones will be set in reference to this stone, thus determining the position of the entire structure !

If you read Genesis, you will see God creating the earth (1:1-13), then we have the rest of creation focusing around the earth (their "purpose").

And God said, "Let there be lights in the vault of the sky to separate the day from the night, and let them

> *serve as signs to mark sacred times, and days and years, and let them be lights in the vault of the sky to give light on the earth." And it was so.*
>
> *God made two great lights — the greater light to govern the day and the lesser light to govern the night. He also made the stars. God set them in the vault of the sky to give light on the earth, to govern the day and the night, and to separate light from darkness. And God saw that it was good.*
>
> *And there was evening, and there was morning — the fourth day.*
>
> — Gen 1:14-19

As it is today, so it was in earlier times that the setting of this very important cornerstone was often done with great ceremony. Thus, the angels sang and rejoiced at its creation! Job 38:7 "…while the morning stars sang together and all the angels shouted for joy."

So if God "hangs the earth on nothing," as Job stated (Job 26:7), then what is the answer to God's question "on what were the footing set?" I'm sure Job had no idea and I certainly can't figure it out. But there are very intelligent people who give it a shot!! Modern science has contradictory "theories" that when put together point to the "laws" of nature that both Newton and Einstein put forth. They also point to what God expressed to Job. (We'll try and take a look at this later, as those more learned than I argue and discuss the universe expanding and shrinking.)

In Job 38:6, God wanted Job to grab onto the fact that He both *established* and *is* the force that holds creation together.

He also points out that from the very beginning, it was He who set the "cornerstone" upon which the rest of creation "will be set in reference to this stone, thus determining the position of the entire structure!" (Genesis 1:14-19)

I believe God comforts both Job and us as He rolls out His blueprints before Job and says, "LOOK, I've got a plan. LOOK at what I've done."

Our God is a God of order. He set the reference point for creation; He wants to both set and "be the cornerstone" in our lives. Thus, it is on the basis of who He is that will determine the entire rest of our lives!!

> *"For I know the plans I have for you,' declares the LORD, 'plans to prosper you and not to harm you, plans to give you hope and a future."*
>
> — Jeremiah 29:11

> *So this is what the Sovereign LORD says: "See, I lay a stone in Zion, a tested stone, a precious cornerstone for a sure foundation; the one who relies on it will never be stricken with panic."*
>
> — Isaiah 26:16

> *Jesus said to them, "Have you never read in the Scriptures: The stone the builders rejected has become the cornerstone; the Lord has done this, and it is marvelous in our eyes."*
>
> — Matthew 21:42

Jesus is 'the stone you builders rejected, which has become the cornerstone.' Salvation is found in no one else, for there is no other name under heaven given to mankind by which we must be saved.
— Acts 4:11-12

Consequently, you are no longer foreigners and strangers, but fellow citizens with God's people and also members of his household, built on the foundation of the apostles and prophets, with Christ Jesus himself as the chief cornerstone. In him the whole building is joined together and rises to become a holy temple in the Lord. And in him you too are being built together to become a dwelling in which God lives by his Spirit.
— Ephesians 2:19-22

Have you put your life in the hands of the Master Builder?

CHAPTER 8:

"Water, Water Everywhere…"[1]

Have you ever stood on the shore of the mighty ocean, watched the waves crashing in, and listened to the pounding of the surf? You can't help but feel small! Stories have been told, books written and movies made, all telling of the beauty, majesty, and awesome power of the sea. Close to 70% of the earth's surface area is covered by water.

In Job 38:8 God directs Job (and us) to the fact that He is not "just the Creator," but also the One who is "in control" and "cares for" His creation as well.

Job 38: 8-11 says, "Or who enclosed the sea with doors When, bursting forth, it went out from the womb; When I made a cloud its garment And thick darkness its swaddling band, And I placed boundaries on it And set a bolt and doors, And I said, 'Thus far you shall come, but no farther; And here shall your proud waves stop?'"

On the second day of creation, God separated the waters above from the waters below. On the third day, He separated the sea from the dry land.

Scholars don't know exactly when Job lived. There are numerous indicators in Scripture and other writing that put him somewhere between Noah and Abraham. This would make him familiar with the "the flood." (Job 22:15-16 says, "Hast thou marked the old way which wicked men have trodden? Which were cut down out of time, whose foundation was overflown with a flood...") (I personally hold to the "worldwide flood," and believe there is more than enough scientific evidence for such a stand.)

Most people just think about the rain for forty days and forty nights. But that's not the whole story. Genesis 7:11 says, "In the six hundredth year of Noah's life, in the second month, on the seventeenth day of the month, on the same day all the fountains of the great deep burst open, and the floodgates of the sky were opened."

For years people have wondered what this meant, and it was often used by biblical skeptics to discredit the concept of a global flood. But once again modern science has unintentionally given us some answers. Science has actually found underground seas far below the surface of the earth. Geologists say there are vast storehouses of water "locked up" in a blue crystalline mineral called ringwoodite.

> *A giant blob of water the size of the Arctic Ocean has been discovered hundreds of miles beneath eastern Asia, scientists report.*
> — *National Geographic*, Feb. 2007

> *Wysession has dubbed the new underground feature the "Beijing anomaly," because seismic wave attenuation was found to be highest beneath the Chinese capital city. Wysession first used the moniker during a presentation of his work at the University of Beijing.*
> — *Live Science*, Feb. 2007

> *A new study suggests that a hidden 'ocean' is nestled in the earth's mantle some 400 miles beneath North America. The hidden reservoir, apparently* <u>locked in</u> *[emphasis added by me] to blue crystalline mineral called ringwoodite, may hold three times as much water that exists in all the world's surface oceans.*
> — *The Huffington Post*, June 2014

> *He gathers the waters of the sea into jars; he puts the deep into storehouses.*
> — Psalm 33:7

> *"Like something out of early 19th century playwright Jules Verne's novel,* Journey to the Center of the Earth — *in which characters stumble across a massive underground basin* — *a team of geologists led by Steven Jacobsen from Northwestern University have found a vast body of water, three times the size of any ocean, located near earth's core."*
> — *Time Magazine,* June 2014

God has set the boundaries of the oceans themselves: "You covered it with the deep as with a garment; The waters were standing above the mountains. At Your rebuke they fled, At the sound of Your thunder they hurried away. The mountains rose; the valleys sank down To the place which You established for them. You set a boundary that they may not pass over, So that they will not return to cover the earth "(Psalm 104:6-9).

When God had the flood waters recede, the seas retreated to their shores and to their underground storehouses where the fountains of the deep are once again "bolted and shut." Genesis 8:2 says, "Also the fountains of the deep and the floodgates of the sky were closed, and the rain from the sky was restrained…"

But one of the real stories God had for Job (and us) is of a different purpose! God isn't just giving Job a science lesson. He wanted to give Job insight into the character of God.

In ancient Near East mythology, the sea represented "chaos," and the "steady unresolved tension between chaos and order."

In Scripture, this is understood as standing in opposition to God and His creation purposes. Yet, God uses "chaos" to bring judgement upon men (the flood and Tower of Babel).

The sea is central to the biblical picture of the universe and ultimately the chaos of this world. The sea is also a tribute to the power of God over chaos. As Creator, God controls the seas, both producing and calming its waves (Isaiah 51:15; Jeremiah 31:35), and keeps it within its boundaries (Proverbs 8:27-29 ; Jeremiah 5:22).

Job's life was in chaos. God, as a loving Father, reminds Job that not only is He in control, but He does so as a loving and caring God. He refers to the vast seas (this seemingly uncontrollable chaos) as but a "newborn child," a "baby" coming out of the womb. He then wraps it in a "garment" in a "swaddling band".[2]

God was letting Job know that in the midst of his trials, "like a child," God had Job in His care. He was in control of Job's life.

So, the next time the chaos of life gets you down, take a look at the ocean or the clouds in the sky. Then think of our Creator, and give thanks, as our loving Father wraps us in His arms.

---

1   *The Rime of the Ancient Mariner* (text of 1834), Samuel Taylor Coleridge

2   Swaddling was an age-old practice of wrapping infants in blankets or similar cloths so that movement of the limbs is tightly restricted. Swaddling bands were then used to further restrict the infant. This formed the clothing of the child until it was about a year old, and its omission would be a token that the child had been abandoned (Ezekiel 16:4). Luke 2:7 refers to Mary wrapping the baby Jesus in swaddling bands.

CHAPTER 9:

"Morning Has Broken…"[3]

I can remember being up in the mountains at sunrise, watching the light work its way down the valley and up the side of the mountains. As the sun rose in the sky, the light revealed the different and various trees, rocks, and streams. The formless landscape of the night would become clear.

In verses 12-15, God asked Job a question about one of those "day to day" occurrences.

> *"Have you ever given orders to the morning, or shown the dawn its place, that it might take the earth by the edges and shake the wicked out of it? The earth takes shape like clay under a seal; its features stand out like those of a garment. The wicked are denied their light, and their upraised arm is broken."*
>
> — Job 38: 12-15 NIV

A better rendering of vs 12 would be, "Have you commanded the morning since your days began?" Basically, God was asking: "Job, have you made the morning to come, even once? I mean, in all the days of your life? Is this even in your power to do?"

We don't exactly know how old Job was at the time of his trials. Job 42:16,17 tells us: "After this, Job lived a hundred and forty years; he saw his children and their children to the fourth generation. And so Job died, an old man and full of years."

Most scholars put Job anywhere between 60-80 years old at the time. Striking the midway point at 70 (which also happens to be the most popular opinion) means there would have been 25,550 sunrises during Job's life!! God asks Job, "Have you EVER controlled, EVEN ONCE, the rising of the sun, or where the sun should come up?"

The sun has risen in the east since the beginning. Every day, on time, every time. It is so regular that it is easily calculated and can be found in the tables of "sunrise and sunset." There are tables that tell the time of sunrise and sunset days, weeks, and even months in advance. No one has EVER tried or succeeded to control the sunrise. It is just one of those aspects of the created order that many see as an "impersonal, perpetual force."

God points out the obvious to Job. The sunrise is out of Job's control!! It has occurred every day since the beginning of time without the input or effort of any man.

Not only can't anyone control when it happens – you cannot "stop the light from spreading across the face of the earth" and say "shine here but not there!" ("…or shown the dawn its place, that it might take the earth by the edges" — which literally means to "cover the complete surface").

As the light exposes everything on the face of the earth, God paints the picture of a "seal." This "seal" was different than the Roman or signet ring we are used to. This "seal" was more like a rolling pin with inscriptions and other items imbedded in it. This "seal" was rolled over a clay sheet, making an imprint of what was on the roller.

Now, picture yourself on a ridge, high in the mountains. You've spent the night, and the sun is just now rising. As the sun works its way up in the sky, light rolls down the valley, revealing the mountains, trees, maybe a stream, some rocks. The rise and fall of the ground becomes clear as the darkness is driven away. The colors and patterns of nature and your surroundings are revealed, like a beautiful tapestry ("… its features stand out like those of a garment").

No matter what time frame or calendar, the laws of nature do not change. God established the rising and setting of the sun as a measuring rod. God gave us "time."

And God said, "Let there be lights in the vault of the sky to separate the day from the night, and let them

> *serve as signs to mark sacred times, and days and years,"*
>
> — Genesis 1:14

There is also a second message in this reminder of God's day-to-day wonder.

> *"As sure as the sun will rise in the morning I will also deal with the wicked."*

God points out to Job, with each new dawn, there will be a little house cleaning. Nothing that happens stays hidden or goes unnoticed. That which was done under the cover of darkness will be put away ("…and shake the wicked out of it? …..The wicked are denied their light, and their upraised arm is broken").

Previously, in chapter 24, Job spoke of the wicked going about their evil ways and that night was as day to them.

> *In the dark they dig into houses, They shut themselves up by day; They do not know the light. For the morning is the same to him as thick darkness, For he is familiar with the terrors of thick darkness.*
>
> — Job 24:16-17

God spoke and light came into being. Light symbolically involves the removal of darkness, in the unfolding of biblical history and theology. Darkness and light are meant to bring forth thoughts and images.

- Darkness = wicked, anti-God, death, judgement.
- Light = the first of the created works, life, salvation, the commandments and Word of God.)

The contrast of light and darkness is common to all the words for "light" in both Old and New Testaments, the literal contrast between good and evil. Nowhere in the Bible will you find that darkness is equal in power to God's light. God is the absolute Sovereign ruler over the darkness and the powers of evil.

The Apostle Paul in 2 Corinthians 4:6 points us back to the creation account: "For God, who said, 'Let light shine out of darkness,' make his light shine in our hearts to give us the light of the knowledge of the glory of God in the face of Christ"

God reminds Job there are those day-by-day occurrences that have been set into motion that he (we) can count on, but Job had absolutely no control. Our ability to count on the sun rising tomorrow applies to God's dealing with men as well.

God will "deny them their light and those that raise their arms (fists) against Him will be struck down."

The course of nature is in God's hands, as well as the course of men's lives.

So the next sunrise you experience, praise the Lord! You can count on Him to always be there "on time – every time." Enjoy the tapestry of His creation!

---

3   Christian Hymn by Eleanor Farjeon, 1931

CHAPTER 10:

"Voyage to the Bottom of the Sea"[4]

In vs 8-11 we looked at the "sea" and what it meant, both as a literal creation and symbolically as chaos. Here in verses

16-18, God again is going to use the "sea." But this time Job is presented with both a physical and metaphysical dilemma.

These are questions that humbled Job and could only be answered with a resounding NO.

Job 38:16-18 says, "Have you journeyed to the springs of the sea or walked in the recesses of the deep? Have the gates of death been shown to you? Have you seen the gates of the deepest darkness? Have you comprehended the vast expanses of the earth? Tell me, if you know all this."

Looking at the first part of the question, I assume Job knew very little about "springs of the sea." Then there is the term "walk in the recesses of the deep," which literally means "to observe that which is only found by searching."

The word for "springs" in Hebrew is NEBEK. This word refers to places where water flows or bursts out of the earth. I'm sure Job had seen many springs on the land but had no experience with undersea springs. In fact, it would have been impossible for Job to have explored the "springs of the sea." God put Job in a place where he had to answer "No." Job had to admit to a limited understanding of the physical world around him.

But our knowledge of the oceans today far surpasses that of Job's, right!! Let's take a look at what modern science "truly" reveals.

Today's scientists have not literally walked these deep waters. But they do explore them with deep-sea submersibles and computer models.

In the 1930s, William Beebe's bathysphere deep sea dives gave us a close look at the ocean floor, but no springs were observed.

In the 1940s, mapping of undersea topography was under way using the "echo sounder." Thousands of undersea volcanoes, called "seamounts" and "guyots," were found, and speculation about undersea springs increased.

Then in the 1960s, metal-rich, hot brines were discovered using sonar in the bottom of the Red Sea. This was indirect evidence of water coming out of the ocean floor! After this, scientists using scuba equipment located shallow-water hot springs along the coast of Baja California.

Deep diving research submarines have now been constructed to withstand the tremendous pressure at the ocean floor. The first direct observations of deep sea springs were made on the Mid-Atlantic Ridge by Project "FAMOUS" in 1973. Hot springs were then discovered.

These "hot springs" were photographed and samples taken from the Galapagos Rift in the Pacific Ocean, in 1977. They were also found on the East Pacific Rise, just south of the California Gulf, in 1979. The East Pacific Rise springs were shown in Science News, January 12, 1980. The article was titled, "Smokers, Red Worms, and Deep Sea Plumbing," and was followed by the caption "Sea floor oases of mineral-rich springs and amazing creatures fulfill oceanographers' dreams."

The discovery of these deep ocean springs has been said to be the "most significant oceanographic find since the discovery of the Mid-Atlantic Ridge."[5]

The water coming out of these under sea "smokers" has been measured at 572° F hotter than the surrounding waters (the first attempt to measure the water temperature melted Alvin's heat probe). The research continues.

In 2003, Andrew Fisher, Professor of Earth and Planetary Sciences at the University of California Santa Cruz, discovered that seawater sinks into the seafloor's crust then rises through vents many miles away.[6] In the report, he wrote, "Ever since we discovered a place where these processes occur, we have been trying to understand what drives the fluid flow, what it looks like, and what determines the flow direction."

When today's scientists study the working that power hydrothermal vents, and we look at Job's "springs of the sea," they inadvertently confirm the accuracy and wisdom that springs forth throughout the Scriptures.

The discovery of ocean springs has been said to rank as one of the foremost scientific accomplishments. (They have found "that which is only found by searching," Job 38:16.) But let us remember, even though these springs were not studied or as understood as they are today, the existence of these "sea springs" can be seen in the book of Job. This was thousands of years ago.

Surely, God spoke through men by means of His Holy Spirit. I believe these springs are mentioned so we can marvel at the wisdom and power of God (Genesis 7:11 and 8:2, Proverbs 8:27-29).

Modern science confirms what God had previously said existed! Something that neither Job nor we could see below the surface, "in the recesses of the deep."

It is by "faith" that we are to take God at His Word. (Hebrews 11:1 says, "Now faith is the assurance of things hoped for, the conviction of things not seen.") But, at the same time, it is to our benefit to seek to understand what we don't understand, "that which is only found by searching."

> *My son, if you accept my words and store up my commands within you, turning your ear to wisdom and applying your heart to understanding — indeed, if you call out for insight and cry aloud for understanding, and if you look for it as for silver and search for it as for hidden treasure, then you will understand the fear of the LORD and find the knowledge of God.*
> — Proverbs 2:1-5 NIV

Happy hunting!

....

4 1961 – 1968 Sci-Fi/Action film/tv series

5 West, Susan, "Smokers, Red Worms, and Deep Sea Plumbing," Science News, V. 117, No. 2, January 12, 1980, pp. 28-30. Corliss, John B., et al., "Submarine Thermal Springs on the Galapagos Rift," Science, V. 203, No. 4385, March 16, 1979, pp. 1073-1083.

6 Stephens, T. *A 'hydrothermal siphon' drives water circulation through the seafloor*. University of California Santa Cruz News. Posted news.ucsc.edu June 26, 2015, accessed June 29, 2015.

CHAPTER 11:

"O Death, Where Is Thy Sting?"[7]

I shall be telling this with a sigh
Somewhere ages and ages hence:
Two roads diverged in a wood, and I —
I took the one less traveled by,
And that has made all the difference.
   — "The Road Not Taken," by Robert Frost

Job 38:17-18 brings us outside of the physical, visible creation. God continues to point Job to his limitations. But He wasn't doing this to make fun of Job or make him "feel bad."

It was quite obvious that Job felt pretty bad as it was! God will often show our limitations in order to show us that He is "limitless"!

2 Corinthians 12:9 says,

> *And He has said to me, "My grace is sufficient for you, for power is perfected in weakness." Most gladly, therefore, I will rather boast about my weaknesses, so that the power of Christ may dwell in me.*

Amos 4:13 says,

> *For behold, He who forms mountains and creates the wind And declares to man what are His thoughts, He who makes dawn into darkness And treads on the high places of the earth, The LORD God of hosts is His name.*

We saw last time that the existence of the "springs of the deep" had been known even in OT times. (Well before they were "discovered" in 1973). Yet even though the existence of these springs was known, no one understood anything about them, until they were "found by searching."

In verses 17 and 18, God points Job to yet another "place", another unknown.

This "place," even though its existence is known and somewhat understood, cannot be "found by searching."

Job 38:17-18 says, "Have the gates of death been shown to you? Have you seen the gates of the deepest darkness? Have you comprehended the vast expanses of the earth? Tell me, if you know all this."

God brackets the metaphysical (the understanding of death and the spiritual world) with the physical (springs of the sea/vast expanses of the earth). In biblical times it was the "most important point" that was put in the middle. This was God saying to Job, "How can you explain what can't be seen, when you can't even fully comprehend what can be seen."

That last part of the question is what puts Job on the spot. The word "comprehend" in Hebrew is "biyn" (pronounced bene or "bean" for us non-Hebrew scholars). It means to "perceive," "understand in the mind," "have insight into," or to "have such an understanding of a subject that you are 'able to teach.'"

If you would allow me to paraphrase these verses they may read like this:

> *"Job, do you know when, where, or how you're going to die?*
>
> *Have you seen and do you understand what is on the other side of death?*
>
> *Do you 'comprehend'? Are you even able to teach Me about the vast expanses of the earth, which you do see?*
>
> *Explain it to Me, if you have all this knowledge."*

Death is an inevitable consequence of life (nothing new there). ALL living things in nature die. (Again, this is not groundbreaking news!!)

This has been a source of concern and curiosity to mankind for centuries. There are numerous books out today talking about "near death experience" and things "beyond the grave."

(Just as a footnote here. NONE of these authors actually died and were buried. I'm still looking for the book written by Lazarus and co-authored by Mary and Martha.)

There are those who seek to oust God, and/or explain everything in "natural terms." They have sought the answer to death and what happens "after a person dies," by turning to "science." "Science and research" will find the answer to these questions.

I looked to see what Science has found. Once again, those who claim to have found a better understanding of what happens at death present their information in such a way that it makes you "think" they've got an answer.

After all, look at ALL THE EVIDENCE!! Data collected by "experts in their field."

Let's take a close look at some of this "evidence."

Here are the results of the "largest medical study ever into near-death experiences." Scientists at the University of Southampton spent *four years* examining more than 2,000 people who suffered cardiac arrests at 15 hospitals in the UK, US, and Austria. They found that nearly 40% of those who survived described some kind of "awareness" during the time when they were clinically dead, before their hearts were restarted.

FACTS from the study that are not put "up front":[8]

- Of 2,060 cardiac arrest patients studied, 330 survived — *Only 16% survived. We are still waiting to hear back from the remaining 84%.*
- Of those (330) that survived, 140 were surveyed — *Only 42%, less than half the survivors, were actually surveyed! This is only 6.8% of the total cardiac arrest patients studied.*
- Of those (140) surveyed, 39% *(again, less than 50% or only 55 people)* said they had experienced some kind of awareness during the time when they were clinically dead, before their hearts were restarted. — *We are now talking about the experiences of 55 people having "some kind of awareness." These 55 people now represent "the largest medical study ever on near-death experience." We are talking 61% or 85 people DID NOT have "some kind of awareness."*

"Many could not recall specific details," but some themes emerged.

- One in five *(that's 20% or 11 people out of 55)* said they had felt an unusual sense of peacefulness. "Others recounted feelings of fear or drowning or being dragged through deep water. — *The "others"= 44 people who either recounted fear, drowning, dragged through deep water or something other than peaceful.*
- Nearly one third *(that's 18 out of 55 people)* said time had slowed down or speeded up. — *That's*

18 people who were divided into two totally opposite experiences of "time". And, 37 people who did not express any change in time.

- "Some" *(no mention of what that number may be!!)* recalled seeing a bright light, a golden flash, or the sun shining.
- Thirteen percent *(7 people out of 55)* said they had felt separated from their bodies, and "the same number said their senses had been heightened." *(Nineteen people, the largest of the three groups, made no mention of either experience.)*

THEREFORE, what can we conclude about life after death from the "evidence" given to us by "the largest medical study ever on the subject of after death experience or life after death" (55 people)?

1. It may be peaceful or dreadful.
2. Time will either speed up or slow down *(or not change at all)*
3. We either leave our bodies or stay in them with our senses heightened *(or no sensation mentioned)*

Question: Why are these numbers presented by scientists as they are?

Simple. It doesn't make for a good scientific report after four years of "the largest medical study ever" to say THE MAJORITY of those surveyed didn't reveal anything !!!!!

Mankind has been looking at and thinking about death and the afterlife probably longer than any other natural occurrences. Yet, without God, and left to his own ability to understand, we are still with uncertainty.

So, where does that leave us (and Job) on this matter? The phrase "pulai hadou" is a Jewish expression meaning "realm of the dead" and has also been translated "gates of hell." These are the same two words that appear in the Septuagint version of Job 38:17, "Have the gates of death been revealed to you, or have you seen the gates of deep darkness [puloroi de hadou]?"

They also appear in Isaiah 38:10. In both examples, pulai hadou is a representation for death. These gates represent the passageway from this life to the grave.

Now, I think it's safe to say, Job was "depressed." (Although he didn't follow his wife's advice to curse God and die!) In several chapters we read how Job cursed the day he was born. He also questioned the reason for a life of suffering.

> *After this, Job opened his mouth and cursed the day of his birth.*
>
> —Job 3:1

> *Why is light given to those in misery, and life to the bitter of soul, to those who long for death that does not come, who search for it more than for hidden treasure, who are filled with gladness and rejoice when they reach the grave? Why is life given to a man whose way is hidden, whom God has hedged in? ....*
>
> —Job 3:20-26

I despise my life; I would not live forever. Let me alone; my days have no meaning.

—Job 7:16

I loathe my very life; therefore I will give free rein to my complaint and speak out in the bitterness of my soul.

—Job 10:1

If only I had never come into being, or had been carried straight from the womb to the grave! Are not my few days almost over? Turn away from me so I can have a moment's joy before I go to the place of no return, to the land of gloom and utter darkness, to the land of deepest night, of utter darkness and disorder, where even the light is like darkness.

—Job 10:19-22

But Job had a realistic view of life and eternity.

A person's days are determined; you have decreed the number of his months and have set limits he cannot exceed.

—Job 14:5

But a man dies and is laid low; he breathes his last and is no more. As the water of a lake dries up or a riverbed becomes parched and dry, so he lies down and

> *does not rise; till the heavens are no more, people will not awake or be roused from their sleep.*
>
> —Job 14:10-12

> *I know that my redeemer lives, and that in the end he will stand on the earth. And after my skin has been destroyed, yet in my flesh I will see God; I myself will see him with my own eyes — I and not another. How my heart yearns within me!*
>
> —Job 19:25-27

So if God wasn't revealing something new about death, what was He saying?

Gates are often used to denote a "secured or fortified entrance." At the gates of ancient cities, courts of justice were frequently held, and hence "judges of the gate" are spoken of (Deuteronomy 16:18; 17:8; 21:19; 25:677). At the gates, prophets also frequently delivered their messages (Proverbs 1:21; 8:3; Isaiah 29:21; Jeremiah 17:19-20; 26:10) Criminals were punished outside the gates (1 Kings 21:13; Acts 7:59).

Job was not only a very wealthy and righteous man, but he also held a very influential position in his community. Job often sat at the city gates as a judge and counselor.

> *When I went to the gate of the city and took my seat in the public square, the young men saw me and stepped aside and the old men rose to their feet; the chief men refrained from speaking and covered their mouths with their hands; the voices of the nobles were*

hushed, and their tongues stuck to the roof of their mouths.

Whoever heard me spoke well of me, and those who saw me commended me, because I rescued the poor who cried for help, and the fatherless who had none to assist them. The one who was dying blessed me; I made the widow's heart sing.

I put on righteousness as my clothing; justice was my robe and my turban. I was eyes to the blind and feet to the lame. I was a father to the needy; I took up the case of the stranger. I broke the fangs of the wicked and snatched the victims from their teeth.

I thought, "I will die in my own house, my days as numerous as the grains of sand. My roots will reach to the water, and the dew will lie all night on my branches. My glory will not fade; the bow will be ever new in my hand."

People listened to me expectantly, waiting in silence for my counsel. After I had spoken, they spoke no more; my words fell gently on their ears. They waited for me as for showers and drank in my words as the spring rain. When I smiled at them, they scarcely believed it; the light of my face was precious to them. I chose the way for them and sat as their chief; I dwelt as a king among his troops; I was like one who comforts mourners.

—Job 29:7-25

Here, God brings Job to another set of gates, the gates of death and deep darkness. Job recognized that even if he still had all his wealth, status, and influence, he has no seat or position when it comes to the gates of death. Job has come full circle, remembering life in "the good ol' days" and despairing about life in his present situation.

(Chapter 21, "I thought, 'I will die in my own house, my days as numerous as the grains of sand. My roots will reach to the water, and the dew will lie all night on my branches. My glory will not fade; the bow will be ever new in my hand.'")

Job realized that he had no say in the matter. Job has no seat at the gates of death.

So, we listen in on God's conversation with Job. We look at the "vast expanse of the earth" and learn of "that which can only be found by searching." We are left in the same place God has Job.

None of us knows when, where or how we are going to die.

BUT, concerning what happens after death, we have a decision to make.

Jesus said, "Enter through the narrow gate; for the gate is wide and the way is broad that leads to destruction, and there are many who enter through it" (Matthew 7:13).

I've chosen the road "less traveled by, and that has made all the difference." How about you?

----

7   1 Corinthians 15:55

8   All italics are mine for emphasis or commentary.

CHAPTER 12:

"Where Do You Live?"

And God said, "Let there be light," and there was light. God saw that the light was good, and he separated the light from the darkness.

— Genesis 1:3-4

Have you ever thought about light? How about darkness? The next few verses are some of the deepest questions that we can dive into. God continues to point Job back to the very beginning of creation.

God asks what seem to be a couple of "pretty abstract questions." But to Job they made perfect sense.

Like the "springs of the sea" or the "gates of death,"; Job would have been familiar with what God was asking, but without any firsthand knowledge.

> *What is the way to the abode of light? And where does darkness reside? Can you take them to their places? Do you know the paths to their dwellings? Surely you know, for you were already born! You have lived so many years!*
>
> —Job 38:19-21

Ask yourself the question; "Where does light come from?" If you remember back to grade school, you were taught that the sun is the closest star and provides light and heat to the earth. I can even remember being told, "Without the energy from the sun, there would be no life on earth." At night we can see the moon and light from stars that are far-far away.

Soooo, if you were asked, "What is the way to the abode of light?" you'd point to the sun and say, "That way!"

Well, when God used the phrases "abode," "reside," "their places," and "their dwellings," He was really asking Job for their point of origin or their place of birth.

God was saying "Can you give someone directions or explain where light and darkness exist?"

"How is that different than the sun and the stars?" you ask. "Didn't God in the beginning create the sun and the stars to give light and divide day and night?"

And, the answer would be, "Yes." BUT your answer to God's question would be wrong.

Let's look through Job's eyes.

Scholars and historians will tell you almost every culture or religion has a creation story, BUT, few will point out that the Hebrew (or Biblical) creation story has a unique feature to it! You see, God created "light" in Genesis 1:3 (the first day). He made the plants on the "third day." He created the sun, moon, and stars (vs.14-17) on the "fourth day" (after "light" on the first day and the plants which He made on the third day)

The text forces us to understand that light came before the sun. This shows the writer of Genesis did not copy from other creation stories, because all others had the sun as the source of all light.

> *It was inconceivable to pagan thinking that life could exist without the sun and its light. Hence pagan religions worshiped the sun as the source of light and heat ... The Bible is unique in stating that the sun is of secondary importance ...*
> — Donald Chittick, *The Controversy*, Portland, Oregon: Multnomah Press, 1984, p. 151

This Hebrew story is unique, for only the Hebrews believed light came before the sun.

Also, the Hebrew words used here in Genesis 1:3 give us a clue in the creation account. When God created "light" in verse 3, the word used is associated with the "presence of light" or "light itself." The word used for "lights" (on Day #4) is best translated "light bearers." Their purpose was not only to give light, but to serve as timekeepers for man once he was created.

(For semi-creationists who claim that the "days" of Genesis 1 must have been long periods of time, a more serious problem arises. Genesis plainly teaches that plants appeared on Day #3, and the sun on Day #4. But plants need sunlight for photosynthesis and cannot wait in darkness for millions of years. If the days were long epochs, as demanded by critics of a literal Creation Week, plants could not have survived! I think it's strangely funny how God did things in such a way that you can't explain away what He has said and what He has done.)

So, what was Job looking at here? God was talking about DAY #1! YOU CANT GET ANY MORE BEGINNING THAN THIS!! Hence God's pointed statement, "...Surely you know, for you were already born!..."

There are several thoughts on how God did this. I can't possibly cover them all, but I will share with you what I believe to be a good explanation.

To unravel a possible explanation (since none of us were there either!), we have to take a look at Day #2.

> *And God said, "Let there be a vault between the waters to separate water from water." So God made the vault and separated the water under the vault from the water above it. And it was so. God called the vault "sky." And there was evening, and there was morning — the second day.*
>
> *— Genesis 1:6-8*

This "vault/expanse/firmament" that God called "sky" refers to "the visible heavens above" or "the abode of the stars." (As we saw previously with modern science, "visible" heavens has grown to become pretty big! This vault or "sky" is also far more than the earth's atmosphere and the clouds over our heads, since we'll see that God hung the sun and the stars in this same expanse.)

This is the intent of the verses:

- Psalm 104:2 (NIV) "The LORD wraps himself in light as with a garment; He stretches out the heavens like a tent."
- Isaiah 40:22 (NIV) "He sits enthroned above the circle of the earth, and its people are like grasshoppers. He stretches out the heavens like a canopy, and spreads them out like a tent to live in."
- Isaiah 34:4 (NIV) "All the stars in the sky will be dissolved and the heavens rolled up like a scroll; all the starry host will fall like withered leaves from the vine, like shriveled figs from the fig tree."
- Revelation 6:14 (NIV) "The heavens receded like a scroll being rolled up, and every mountain and island was removed from its place."

Picture God creating the earth and "light" on the first day. He then encompassed the earth in a "tent" or "vault." He spread the firmament around the earth and underneath the light. He created the sun, moon, and stars and placed them inside this tent.

And God said, "Let there be lights in the vault of the sky to separate the day from the night, and let them serve as signs to mark sacred times, and days and years, and let them be lights in the vault of the sky to give light on the earth." And it was so.

God made two great lights — the greater light to govern the day and the lesser light to govern the night. He also made the stars. God set them in the vault of the sky to give light on the earth, to govern the day and the night, and to separate light from darkness. And God saw that it was good. And there was evening, and there was morning — the fourth day.

— Genesis 1: 14-19

Do you get the picture?

- The earth is covered in darkness (vs 2. "darkness was over the surface of the deep"). God then created "light"[9] and bathed the earth with it, separating the darkness.
- Day #2 — He creates the "sky" (vault/firmament/expanse).
- Day #3 — God is really on a roll. He creates the seas and dry land, then all plant life.
- Day #4 — God created the "light bearers" and they were given to us to govern time, seasons, etc. This makes the light of day #1 entirely different than the lights on day #4.

What does "science" say about all this?

- "The radiation (light) being described here is not coming out of any kind of matter — the usual

source of light energy. The region around the black hole is quite empty of matter. Instead, this radiation is coming out of empty space itself!"
— P. C. Davies, "Uncensoring the Universe", *The Sciences*, March/April 1977, p. 7)

- Scientists create light from vacuum. — Phys.org Nov. 27, 2011
- Physicists create light out of nothing.[10] — ABC Science, Nov. 17, 2011
- The speed of light in a vacuum is constant, according to Einstein's theory of relativity. But its speed passing through any given material depends on a property of that substance known as its index of refraction. By varying a material's index of refraction, researchers can influence the speed at which both real and virtual photons travel within it. — *Scientific American* Feb. 12, 2013 "Something from Nothing? A Vacuum Can Yield Flashes of Light"

If modern scientific theory claims the possibility of light coming out of empty space (in other words, without light bearing objects), how can we criticize the biblical idea that light existed on the first day of creation without sun, moon, or stars?

The fact that Genesis talks about light existing before the appearance of the sun, moon, and stars seem rather to be evidence of divine authorship of the Bible!

We must also note that the Bible says there will be light in the future New Jerusalem without the sun. Since there will be no need for the sun as a light source in the future, it is certainly possible that there was no need for the sun as a light source in the beginning.

> *The sun shall no longer be your light by day, nor for brightness the moon shall give light to you; but the Lord will be your everlasting light.*
>
> — Isaiah 60:19

> *And there shall be no night there: They shall need no lamp nor light of the sun, for the Lord God gives them light. And they shall reign for ever and ever.*
>
> — Revelation 22:5

God does everything for a reason! He often profoundly points out several important facts in a simple single statement.

Creation serves just such a purpose. BEFORE mankind was created, BEFORE Job or any of us were conceived, God was busy designing and bringing into existence a Creation that ultimately points to Him!!

GOD is the source. If we were to look for where light dwells and the abode of darkness. We would be looking for God. He is where light dwells and holds the abode of darkness.

Job, do you know the way?

Thankfully God has given us directions:

> *And Jesus said, "I am the light of the world."*
>
> — John 8:12 NIV

> *Jesus said to him, "I am the way, and the truth, and the life; no one comes to the Father but through Me."*
>
> — John 14:6

> *And you know the way where I am going.*
>
> — John 14:4

So each day as you watch the sun rise and set, as you look into the vastness of the night sky and see the stars, can you say, "I know where the light dwells"? Or are you living in darkness?

....

9   There are those that say the "light" from Day #1 "refers to God," since "God is light."

"This is the message we have heard from him and declare to you: God is light; in him there is no darkness at all." — 1 John 1:5 NIV

"And Jesus said, 'I am the light of the world.'" — John 8:12 NIV)

We have to be very careful here, because God created "light." HE DID NOT CREATE JESUS. Therefore, the "light" on Day #1 does not refer to God, but simply "light itself" as a creation by God.

10 According to the First Law of Thermodynamics, nothing in the universe (i.e., matter or energy) can pop into existence from nothing (see Miller, 2013). "All" of the scientific evidence points to that conclusion. So, the universe could not have popped into existence before the alleged "Big Bang" (an event which I do not endorse). Therefore, God must have created the universe.

One of the popular rebuttals given by the atheistic community is that "quantum mechanics could have created the universe."

In 1905, Albert Einstein proposed the idea of mass-energy equivalence, resulting in the famous equation $E = mc^2$ (1905). We now know that matter can be converted to energy, and vice versa. However, energy and mass are conserved in keeping with the First Law.

In the words of the famous evolutionary astronomer, Robert Jastrow, "[T]he principle of the conservation of matter and energy… states that matter and energy can be neither created nor destroyed. Matter can be converted into energy, and vice versa, but the total amount of all matter and energy in the universe must remain unchanged forever" (1977, p. 32). The idea of matter-energy conversion led one physicist to postulate, in essence, that the cosmic egg that exploded billions of years ago in the alleged "Big Bang" — commencing the "creation" of the universe — could have come into existence as an energy-to-matter conversion.

In 1973, physicist Edward Tryon of the Hunter College of the City University of New York published a paper in the British science journal *Nature* titled, "Is the Universe a Vacuum Fluctuation?" Tryon proposed the idea that the Universe could be a large-scale vacuum energy fluctuation. He said, "In answer to the question of why it happened, I offer the modest proposal that our universe is simply one of those things which happens from time to time." (246:397)

Does it really? Is this the "scientific" explanation?

It is easier to accept Scripture as it stands. God's creation and His work in our lives doesn't always need to be (nor can they be) fully understood and explained (by modern scientific thought). What does need to happen is for us to believe and obey.

CHAPTER 13:

Seeing Things as "Black or Light"

What is the way to the abode of light? And where does darkness reside? Can you take them to their places? Do you know the paths to their dwellings? Surely you know, for you were already born! You have lived so many years!

—Job 38:19-21

Previously we took a look at the "light from Day #1." Now I want to take a look at "darkness."

In Job 38:19-21, God doesn't talk to Job as if darkness is "just the absence of light." The Bible presents it as something entirely different. God speaks to Job about "Light" and "Darkness" as two separate and identifiable things: "Can you take them to their places?" and "Do you know the paths to their dwellings?"

There are those who say, "This is all figurative or symbolic language." But if we say that there is such a thing as "light" — if we acknowledge through our senses and knowledge that light is an actual physical part of the creation of God — we have no problem recognizing that "light can be a symbol of 'goodness.'"

If a "symbol" is to be recognized, it must be based on something that is tangible and real. Even the mythological creatures of some cultures are designed and based on something "real." To say "an ox is a symbol of strength" to someone that has neither seen nor knows what an ox looks like would be meaningless! A unicorn with wings is based upon a horse and an eagle and a horned animal. To explain a unicorn to someone who has never seen nor understands what a horse is would be futile. A symbol has to be "recognizable" and understood.

This being true, how can we turn around and say, "darkness is not real" or "darkness is just the absence of light" and that "darkness symbolizes evil." Darkness is real and a recognizable state.

Both "light" and "darkness" are spoken of in vs.19-21 IN THE SAME CONTEXT.

If you say, "darkness is the absence of light," why can't you say, "light is the absence of darkness"?

Now, before you get upset at me and think I'm taking this way too far; remember we are talking Day #1 (pre-firmament, pre-sun, moon, and stars). We are looking at "modern science" which has discovered the existence of "light from nothing" and "without a light source.". Scientists are now talking about "dark matter."

> "Roughly 80 percent of the mass of the universe is made up of material that scientists cannot directly observe. This discovery called "dark matter"[11], this bizarre ingredient does not emit light or energy...
>
> "Studies of other galaxies in the 1950s first indicated that the universe contained more matter than seen by the naked eye. Support for dark matter has grown, and although no solid direct evidence of dark matter has been detected, there have been strong possibilities in recent years.
>
> "Scientists calculate the mass of large objects in space by studying their motion. Astronomers examining spiral galaxies in the 1950s expected to see material in the center moving faster than on the outer edges. Instead, they found the stars in both locations traveled at the same velocity, indicating the galaxies contained more mass than could be seen. Studies of the gas within elliptical galaxies also indicated a need for more mass than found in visible objects. Clusters of galaxies would fly apart if the only mass they contained were visible to conventional astronomical

measurements. Albert Einstein showed that massive objects in the universe bend and distort light, allowing them to be used as lenses. By studying how light is distorted by galaxy clusters, astronomers have been able to create a map of dark matter in the universe.

"All of these methods provide a strong indication that most of the matter in the universe is something yet unseen."

— "What is Dark Matter?" by Nola Taylor Redd, Space.com Contributor | June 15, 2017

God created the heavens and the earth "and darkness was over the surface of the deep." Darkness was a product of God's initial creation of the heavens and the earth. When it was still "formless and empty." (Isaiah 45:7 "I form the light and create darkness, I bring prosperity and create disaster; I, the LORD, do all these things.") In God's statement here, we can clearly say that the act of forming the light does not create darkness — because the act of bringing prosperity does not create disaster!! God is pointing out that He is the One that brings BOTH into play.

- He then said, "Let there be light."
- He also saw that the light was good. (This is a key point that I will discuss next time.)
- He "separated or divided" the light from the darkness. The word used here means to "keep apart or force apart, disconnect, to break apart into individual units or components." You don't

physically separate a "real, created item" from an "imaginary, figurative or 'purely symbolic'" item!
- Darkness is a real thing.

Then the LORD said to Moses, "Stretch out your hand toward the sky so that darkness spreads over Egypt — darkness that can be felt." So Moses stretched out his hand toward the sky, and total darkness covered all Egypt for three days. No one could see anyone else or move about for three days. Yet all the Israelites had light in the places where they lived.
— Exodus 10: 21-23

The people remained at a distance, while Moses approached the thick darkness where God was.
— Exodus 20:21

The LORD reigns, let the earth be glad; let the distant shores rejoice. Clouds and thick darkness surround him; righteousness and justice are the foundation of his throne.
— Psalms 97:1-2

From noon until three in the afternoon darkness came over all the land.
— Matthew 27:45

God then separates light and darkness, by assigning to each its relative position in time and space ("their dwellings").

This no doubt refers to "day" and "night," as we learn from the following verse. And the very "first day" was designated.

We can take a look at what all this meant to Job. Next time. Until then:

> *But if we walk in the light, as he is in the light, we have fellowship with one another, and the blood of Jesus, his Son, purifies us from all sin.*
>
> — 1 John 1:7 NIV

---

11 Emphasis added.

CHAPTER 14:

"Can You Tell Me How to Get to…?" *or* "Good Day"

What is the way to the abode of light? And where does darkness reside? Can you take them to their places? Do you know the paths to their dwellings? Surely you know, for you were already born! You have lived so many years.

— Job 38:19-21 (NIV)

Just a reminder: we are dealing with Day #1. I keep getting the impression that God often wants us to "begin at the beginning" when it comes to facing those hard times and difficult decisions.

Day #1 could possibly be one of the most crucial happenings, as God lays out His plans for Creation. Therefore, I believe it should play a role in how we think.

> "Surely you know, for you were already born! You have lived so many years!"

This is God's counter statement to Job's "I wasn't born yesterday" thinking. (Job 30:1 "But now they mock me, men younger than I, whose fathers I would have disdained to put with my sheep dogs.")

Age was very important when it came to respect and an expectation of wisdom plus experience. Job was older than his so-called comforters and therefore expected a more "respectful" approach to his situation and his remarks.

God simply reminded Job that even in his advanced years and position, he was not there in the beginning and therefore did not play a role in deciding the outcome.

> "Where is the way to the dwelling of light, and where is the place of darkness, that you may take it to its territory and that you may discern the paths to its home?"

Here God is asking Job about "the place of origin" or the "source," their "place of birth."

God IS THE BEGINNING. We all know that, and Job knew that also. But sometimes when we're facing difficulties (as Job certainly was) we need to BEGIN our thoughts with that fact.

We all learn things over the years. We learn from trial and error, personal experiences, or from those that have a particular knowledge of a subject. But no amount of time, trials and errors, personal experiences, or innumerable councilors can replace the knowledge of God.

> *And he said to man, "Behold, the fear of the Lord, that is wisdom, and to turn away from evil is understanding."*
>
> — Job 28:28

Yet, there is a second major point in bringing Job back to the beginning. Just as the ocean or sea represented "chaos," and God was in control, in the same way, both light and darkness carry with them the images of "right and wrong," "good and bad."

Here God puts forth a very important truth. If He is the beginning and the source, then it stands to reason God decides what is GOOD!!

The very first time God referred to something as "good" was in Genesis 1:4. This is the very first time the word "good" was used.

God made a choice, a decision to differentiate between light and darkness. He made a distinction based on something other than their physical nature. He made this distinction even <u>before</u> He separated them physically.

God "saw" the light was good! This was a statement that said "This pleases Me." "I like this." "This makes Me happy." "Nice!" "Ya… this is good!!" It wasn't just a physical observation but a pronouncement!

From here on "light" is often used as a symbol of those thing that are pleasing to God, the right thing to do.

In vs. 4 God drew a dividing line. He set up and established contrast and opposites.

Nature is full of them. Up vs Down, Left vs Right, North vs South, East vs West; the list goes on and on. And like the saying from Campus Crusade for Christ, "Just like there are laws that govern the physical universe, so there are laws that govern the Spiritual realm."

In pointing Job (and us) back to Day #1, to the origin, to the dwellings and birthplace of Light and Darkness, God is having Job think about several facts:

1. God was the beginning of everything. (You weren't there.)
2. God is the One that declares what is "good." God is the one that draws the dividing line. Light and darkness, good and evil do NOT "cohabitate." (He gives them separate designations, "abode of light" and "where darkness resides.")
3. He is the One that separates and marks the differences between good and evil.

This dividing line, this separation between light and dark, between good and evil, this is the battle line. This is the line that God defends and Satan wanted Job (and us) to cross.

> *"Does Job fear God for nothing?" Satan replied. "Have you not put a hedge around him and his household and everything he has? You have blessed the work of his hands, so that his flocks and herds are spread throughout the land. But now stretch out your hand and strike everything he has, and he will surely curse you to your face."*
>
> —Job 1:9-11

> *"Skin for skin!" Satan replied. "A man will give all he has for his own life. But now stretch out your hand and strike his flesh and bones, and he will surely curse you to your face."*
>
> —Job 2:4-5

This is the line Satan wants us to step over. Society (Satan) today wants to blur that line — to say that "we decide" where that line is, that "we decide" what is right and wrong for us. Society (Satan) would even have us believe that there is no such thing and good and evil. Society says "If they do exist — they are of equal value or strength."

Satan's game plan has not changed since the beginning.

> *"You will not certainly die"* (there is no wrong here), *the serpent said to the woman. "For God knows that when you eat from it your eyes will be opened, and you*

will be like God, knowing good and evil." (You can decide what is right.)

— Genesis 3:4-5

Woe to those who call evil good and good evil, who put darkness for light and light for darkness, who put bitter for sweet and sweet for bitter.

— Isaiah 5:20

Job, in his frantic efforts to defend himself from his "comforters," was walking the line. Job was saying "This isn't right. Why is this happening to me, I haven't done anything to deserve this."

God leads Job to understand that he didn't have the knowledge, ability, or authority to direct and decide the course of life.

So the next time you wonder or question "What is the right thing to do?" go back to Day #1. Look at the light, and trace it back to its birth.

Then listen to the One that called it "good."

Your word is a lamp to my feet and a light to my path.
— Psalm 119:105

CHAPTER 15:
"Stormy Weather" *or* "There Will Be a Day"

"Have you entered the storehouses of the snow or seen the storehouses of the hail, which I reserve for times of trouble, for days of war and battle?

What is the way to the place where the lightning is dispersed, or the place where the east winds are scattered over the earth? Who cuts a channel for the torrents of rain, and a path for the thunderstorm, to water a land where no one lives, an uninhabited desert, to satisfy a desolate wasteland and make it sprout with grass? Does the rain have a father? Who fathers the drops of dew? From whose womb comes the ice? Who gives birth to the frost from the heavens when the waters become hard as stone, when the surface of the deep is frozen?"

— Job 38:22-30

In these next several verses, we have a lot more than God talking to Job about the weather.

Here in New England, we normally don't think of winter in the Middle East, but they do get snow.

The occurrence of snow differs considerably in such varying altitudes. At Jerusalem snow often falls to the depth of a foot or more in January or February, but it doesn't stay. In Nazareth it falls more frequently and deeply, and it has even been known to fall in the maritime plain of Joppa and Carmel. In 2 Samuel 23:20, Samuel gives an account of snow actually falling. (There is another account given in 1 Maccabees 13:22 of the Apochrypha.) But, in the poetical books numerous verses leave no doubt it was an ordinary occurrence in the winter months (see Psalm 147:16; 148:8). In the highest ridges and ravines of Lebanon, snow can be found far into the summer months, and never really disappears. (Jeremiah 18:14 Does the snow of Lebanon ever vanish from its rocky slopes? Do its cool waters from distant sources ever stop flowing?) The summit of Mt. Hermon is perpetually capped with frozen snow. It was from these sources the Jews obtained their supplies of ice for the purpose of cooling their beverages in summer (Proverbs 25:13).

As far back as the times of Job and up to the present, people often refer to the difficult times in our lives as "stormy weather" or "winter months". In the Gospel of Matthew, Christ speaks of the Jews fleeing during the final tribulation and says, "And pray that your flight be not in the winter (which would make their escape difficult and tempt one to delay their escape), neither on the sabbath day" (which may cause some to remain for fear of breaching the sabbath rest Matthew 24:20)

Snow was not just a part of "bad weather" but also a symbol of purity or cleanliness. (See Job 9:30, Psalm 51:7, Isaiah 1:18, Daniel 7:9, Matthew 28:3.) God is going to judge and clean things up!!!

It may seem strange that God is talking to Job "out of the storm" about stormy weather. But God uses a key phrase to direct Job, as He brings up those troubling winter months.

"Which I reserve for times of trouble, for days of war and battle?" God was once again reminding Job, as He did in vs 13, that He intends to deal with and judge those that rebel against Him.

There are numerous occasions in Scripture where God brought storms, snow, hail, lightning, and winds to judge.

> *He sends his command to the earth; his word runs swiftly. He spreads the snow like wool and scatters the frost like ashes. He hurls down his hail like pebbles. Who can withstand his icy blast. He sends his word and melts them; he stirs up his breezes, and the waters flow. He has revealed his word to Jacob, his laws and*

decrees to Israel. He has done this for no other nation; they do not know his laws. Praise the LORD.

— Psalm 147:15-20

Hail is frequently a tool of judgment against God's enemies. We see this against Egypt (Exodus 9:24), the Canaanites (Joshua 10:11), apostate Israel (Isaiah 28:2), Gog and Magog (Ezekiel 38:22), and against a rebellious earth in the Great Tribulation (Revelation 16:20-21).

In Exodus 9:18-26, we read:

"Therefore, at this time tomorrow I will send the worst hailstorm that has ever fallen on Egypt, from the day it was founded till now. Give an order now to bring your livestock and everything you have in the field to a place of shelter, because the hail will fall on every person and animal that has not been brought in and is still out in the field, and they will die."

Those officials of Pharaoh who feared the word of the LORD hurried to bring their slaves and their livestock inside. But those who ignored the word of the LORD left their slaves and livestock in the field.

Then the LORD said to Moses, "Stretch out your hand toward the sky so that hail will fall all over Egypt — on people and animals and on everything growing in the fields of Egypt."

When Moses stretched out his staff toward the sky, the LORD sent thunder and hail, and lightning flashed down to the ground. So the LORD rained hail on the land of Egypt; hail fell and lightning flashed

> back and forth. It was the worst storm in all the land of Egypt since it had become a nation. Throughout Egypt hail struck everything in the fields — both people and animals; it beat down everything growing in the fields and stripped every tree. The only place it did not hail was the land of Goshen, where the Israelites were.

Yet, as deadly as this storm was, this hail cannot compare to the storm that God has in store for the Tribulation. Revelation 16:21 "From the sky huge hailstones, each weighing about a hundred pounds, fell on people. And they cursed God on account of the plague of hail, because the plague was so terrible."

Let's examine this horrific event:

Supercell storms are large, severe, quasi-steady-state storms that form where wind speed or wind direction varies with height (this is what can be referred to as wind shears) and they have separate downdrafts and updrafts (where the associated precipitation is not falling through the updraft) with a strong, rotating updraft called a mesocyclone. These storms normally have such powerful updrafts that the top of the supercell storm cloud (or anvil) can break through the troposphere and reach into the lower levels of the stratosphere. Supercell storms can sometimes be up to 15 miles wide. Research has shown that at least 90 percent of these storms can produce destructive tornadoes (sometimes F3 or higher). They can also produce extremely large hailstones (four inches diameter). Straight-line winds in excess of 81 mph have been measured, with flash floods. In fact, research has also shown that most tornadoes occur from this type of thunderstorm. Supercells are the strongest type of thunderstorm.

The largest hailstone recorded in the United States fell on July 23, 2010, in Vivian, South Dakota. It was eight inches in diameter and weighed 1 pound, 15 ounces (almost two pounds). The other big factor is wind. Depending on the direction of the wind, it can slow or speed up the velocity. A third factor is the shape of the hailstone, because different shapes create different amounts of air resistance.

NOW let's take a look at a 100 pound hailstone!!

- A US liquid gallon of water weighs about 8.34 pounds. (100 pounds = 11.99 gallons of water.) To get a picture of this, think of the big water bottle on the top of a water cooler. This water bottle is normally 5 gallons, so a 100 lb hailstone would be 2.4 water bottles. There are 7.48 gallons in 1 cubic foot, so 100 pounds = 11.99 gallons = about 1.6 cubic feet.
- Plugging in the numbers and assuming a spherical shape (the most common) a 100 lb hailstone at 1.6 cubic feet would reach a terminal velocity of a whopping 217 mph. This in turn gives it a force of impact around 10,800 lbs. (Now that's gotta hurt!!)

God goes on, in the form of rhetorical questions, to present Himself as the "father" of this storm. ("Does the rain have a father? Who fathers the drops of dew? From whose womb comes the ice? Who gives birth to the frost from the heavens when the waters become hard as stone, when the surface of the deep is frozen?") The answer is yes — Jehovah. (Genesis 2:5-6 tells us, "Now no shrub had yet appeared on the earth and no plant had yet sprung up, for the LORD God had not sent rain on the earth and there was no one to work the ground, but a mist came up from the earth and watered the whole surface of the ground.")

We as earthly fathers often fall short of who God intended us to be. But God, who is the perfect Father, completely fulfills what the symbol of what Father means.

So what does a father represent?

- The father was the "pro-genitor" (the beginning, the origin of a particular species, race, or lineage).
- A father was the head of the family, the decision maker. When a decision needed to be made, "The buck stopped there."

If we look again, we can see the similarities in Revelation 16 and the storms that God speaks about to Job, the lightning, the wind and rain and hail. In this conversation with Job, God was telling him:

> *Job, you want to see justice. Well, I'm the one. There will be a day when I'm going to wage war with and bring an end to the rebellion. I'm the Father, and I will act. The decision is Mine with no involvement of men ("to water a land where no one lives, an uninhabited desert, to satisfy a desolate wasteland*

and make it sprout with grass?") My wrath is being "stored up." But the injustice that you see now will come to an end.

As Job was going through stormy times, some winter weather, God says, "Look at My creation — I was there in the beginning, I'm here now, and I've planned ahead to take care of things in the future."

> It was you who set all the boundaries of the earth; you made both summer and winter.
>
> — Psalm 74:17

> Like snow in summer or rain in harvest, honor is not fitting for a fool.
>
> — Proverbs 26:1

> That which is given by the Spirit to the prophet can refer to the past and to the present as well as to the future.
>
> However, that which is revealed to the prophet finds its inner unity in this — that it all aims to establish the supremacy of Jehovah.
>
> Prophecy views also the detailed events in their relation to the Divine plan, and this latter has for its purpose the absolute establishment of the supremacy of Jehovah in Israel and eventually on the entire earth.
>
> — Von, O. C. (1915).
> Prophecy, Prophets.
> In J. Orr, J. L. Nuelsen,

E. Y. Mullins, & M. O. Evans (Eds.),
The International Standard Bible Encyclopaedia
(Vol. 1–5, p. 2464). Chicago:
The Howard-Severance Company.)

CHAPTER 16:

"Only in the Dark Can You See the Stars" *or* "Connecting the Dots"

Can you bind the chains of the Pleiades, or loose the cords of Orion? Can you lead forth a constellation in its season, And guide the Bear with her satellites? Do you know the ordinances of the heavens, Or fix their rule over the earth?

— Job 38:31-33

I have never been a student of astronomy. The most I've ever done is see the Big and Little Dipper and the North Star. But I do enjoy looking at the stars at night, with the beauty and vastness of the evening sky.

In today's society, reading the stars (and I don't mean fortune tellers!!) has become, for the most part, a lost art. In ancient times, people didn't have pretty calendars on the walls telling them when the next full moon was or what year, month, and day of the week it was. In these "olden days" they didn't have road maps or satellites to give GPS directions as they traveled. From the beginning, God set the sun, moon, and stars in the heavens to give men a sense of time and movement or direction.

Stop and think. If you didn't have a clock, didn't have a calendar, and were not able to communicate with anyone, how would you keep track of time?

If you lived near the equator, it wouldn't be too hard. Day and night are pretty evenly split at 12 hours. But there are no real seasonal differences. If you lived nearer either of the poles, days become more difficult, but the seasonal variations in the length of daytime are extreme.

Next, without a map, compass, road system, or GPS device, how would you know which way to travel? You can find north, south, east, or west by learning a few stars and constellations. Or you can simply pick out a star and follow its movements.

Look for the North Star (Polaris, for you astronomically correct people). This will be the bright star in the constellation and doesn't appear to move in the night sky. Polaris can be found at the end of the Little Dipper. Now to find your latitude. If you don't happen to have a spare sextant in your pocket, extend your arm to the horizon and make a fist. Stack one fist on top of the other till you reach the North Star. Each fist gives you about 10 degrees. By various methods you can get a general idea of where you are or where you are going by using the sun, moon, and stars.

Each culture recognizes the same star patterns, but they are often given different names for different meanings. In biology, using the same Latin names enables different biologists to talk with one another and know they are talking about the same animal. Astronomers use Greek when communicating between each other.

Well, since Job wasn't a Greek, and if we are going to understand what exactly is being said here, we need to look at what a Hebrew understood.

First, Job was familiar with the different constellations, and knew well what God was talking about. Job 9:9, "He is the Maker of the Bear and Orion, the Pleiades and the constellations of the south."

"Can you bind the chains of the Pleiades..."

The Hebrew word is actually translated "a cluster," and was understood to have referenced a very recognized group of six to seven stars. Their appearance on the eastern horizon signals a seasonal change. The name used in modern English translations (Pleiades) is derived from the Greek word plain ("to sail"). This cluster of stars was important in determining the sailing seasons on the Mediterranean Sea. The season of navigation began with their first appearance on the eastern horizon. The unique tightness of this "cluster" is what makes it stand out in the night sky. Modern scientists believe they appear so close together (relatively speaking) because these stars were probably made at the same time and are held tight by their gravitational forces.

- Computer simulations have shown that the Pleiades were probably formed from a compact configuration that resembled the Orion Nebulous. Astronomers estimate that the cluster will survive for about another 250 million years, after which it will disperse due to gravitational interactions with its galactic neighborhood.[12]
- The latest scientific observations suggest that they are all bound together, moving in the same direction, according to Dr. Robert J. Trumpler from the Lick Observatory.
- "…no doubt that the Pleiades are not a temporary or accidental agglomeration of stars, but a system in which the stars are bound together by a close kinship." — unknown author

A possible loose paraphrase to this statement would be: "Hey, Job! You know that cluster of stars that I made! Do you think you could hold them all together for me?"

"… *or loose the cords of Orion?*"

This is a prominent group of stars located on the celestial equator and visible throughout the world. It is one of the most conspicuous and recognizable constellations in the night sky.

The recognized Greek name Orion came from a hunter (or what we would call a warrior) in Greek mythology. Its brightest stars are Rigel (Beta Orionis) and Betelgeuse (Alpha Orionis), a blue-white and a red supergiant respectively. The row of three bright stars (Mintaka, Alnilam, Alnitak) make up Orion's Belt.

The Hebrew word for this constellation is actually "kesil" and can better be rendered "fool." It represented Nimrod, who was a symbol of impiety and folly.

(Genesis 10:8-10) Nimrod was a descendant of Cush, the son of Ham. He was the first who claimed to be a "mighty one in the earth." Babel was the beginning of his kingdom, which he gradually enlarged.

To Job this constellation was a reminder of:

- "Nimrod" — A man that put himself above other men and in opposition to God.
- "Nimrod" — a man that sought to build a kingdom and bring everyone under a one world government (Genesis 11:4).
- "Nimrod" — a "mighty man" who God not only stripped of power and authority, but scattered mankind thus dissolving his kingdom.

"To loose the cords" (some translations say "belt"') was another way of saying "strip them of their armor."

This is what the LORD says to his anointed, to Cyrus, whose right hand I take hold of to subdue nations

> *before him and to strip kings of their armor, to open doors before him so that gates will not be shut…*
>
> — Isaiah 45:1

God was saying "Job, do you remember Nimrod? Are you able to strip the armor from him and subdue the 'mighty', as I was?"

What does "modern science" have to say?

Astronomer Garrett P. Serviss commented on Orion: "At the present time this band consists of an almost perfect straight line, a row of second-magnitude stars about equally spaced and of the most striking beauty. In the course of time, however, the two right-hand stars, Mintaka and Alnilam, will approach each other and form a naked-eye double; but the third, Alnitak, will drift away eastward so that the band will no longer exist."

So basically, Orion is the direct opposite of Pleiades — the stars are actually moving in completely different directions. Therefore, God revealed a truth about these constellations to Job, that no human astronomer could ever observe during his time!! This statement by God can only now after thousands of years be confirmed by modern observations.

> *Can you bind the chains of the Pleiades, or loose the cords of Orion? Can you lead forth a constellation in its season, And guide the Bear with her satellites? Do you know the ordinances of the heavens, Or fix their rule over the earth?*
>
> — Job 38:31-33

In conclusion, what can God tell us from the stars?

Job (insert your name here),
Can you hold the stars together or tear them apart? Can you set the seasons and tell the stars their direction? Can you set the rules to govern the stars or determine their course in the sky?
Job, "that which I have established to give you guidance: That which signals seasons and direction, I will hold together. That which stands in opposition to me and my plans: I will bring to an end."
Job (your name here), once again it's out of your hands and you have no control.

....

12 From Wikipedia

CHAPTER 17:

"And Now, for the Local Forecast" *or* "Can You Do This?"

Can you lift up your voice to the clouds, So that an abundance of water will cover you? Can you send forth lightnings that they may go and say to you, "Here we are"? Who has put wisdom in the innermost being Or given understanding to the mind? Who can count the clouds by wisdom, or tip the water jars of the

heavens, When the dust hardens into a mass and the clods stick together?

— Job 38:34-38

In these next verses God brings the conversation down to my level, plain and simple. God talks to Job not just about predicting the weather but controlling the weather. Previously God reminded Job that he could not control the stars; so how about lowering the ceiling a little and asking about the clouds and the weather?

Man's efforts to control (or have an influence upon) the weather has been evident in almost every "primitive" culture; from witchdoctors to our Native American rain dance.

But, even in these examples, most of these cultures believed that some god or spirit was in control, and their efforts were to appeal to that higher power.

Modern Man has turned away from those "primitive" beliefs and has turned to science for the answer. The first efforts to scientifically control and monitor the weather, generally recognized by the meteorological community as constituting weather modification, occurred in 1948.

Dr. Irving Langmuir first experimented with artificially seeding clouds to produce rain. His experiments showed positive results and sparked tremendous interest in the field. In 1975, the US and Canada entered into an agreement, under the auspices of the United Nations, for the exchange of information on weather modification activity.

Weather modification, particularly hostile weather warfare, was addressed by the United Nations General Assembly Resolution 31/72, TIAS 9614 Convention on the Prohibition of

Military or Any Other Hostile Use of Environmental Modification Techniques.

The Convention was signed in Geneva, on May 18, 1977, entered into force on October 5, 1978, ratified by U.S. President Jimmy Carter on December 13, 1979, and the U.S. ratification deposited at New York, January 17, 1980.

Enacted in 1971, here in the US, the National Oceanic and Atmospheric Administration currently keeps records of weather modification projects on behalf of the Secretary of Commerce. In 2005 and 2007 bills were proposed in both the House and the Senate to establish the Weather Modification Operation and Research Board and to fund weather modification research.

Can we make rain clouds to rain where we want? Theoretically it is possible, but practically it's not possible to make it rain anywhere we want.

The act of weather modification is both difficult and very costly. Cloud seeding has only been successful in areas where clouds already exist, and they have to be the right kind of cloud.

Dr. Terblanche (a weather modification expert at the World Meteorological Organization) stated, "There is no scientific basis to this technology." He also said, "So far, no one knows if rain-seeding really does what its supporters claim. Measuring the success of weather modification projects is like peering through a thick fog — and it always has been."

Patrick Sweeney is chief executive of Weather Modification Inc., the world's largest private aerial cloud-seeding company, based in Fargo, ND. Sweeney himself stated, at the beginning of a five-year project in a drought burdened area of India, that "The hardest part is managing expectations.

People in Maharashtra are hoping for a cure-all to drought. They come out and dance in the streets when it rains, they hug our pilots and say, 'Do it again.' But we can't guarantee that the clouds will be there — and willing to cooperate." Sweeney later went on to say that the total success of their efforts as an industry was anywhere between 20-60%. He related it to a cancer patient given a choice of trying a treatment or not, and said, "Most people would accept those odds in light of the alternative."

(True, desperate people often do desperate things. But in day-to-day life would you take your car to a mechanic that offered you a 20-60% chance of fixing your car, in the best of circumstances? How about buying a brand new phone giving you a 20-60% chance that it would work, at best? — these are just my thoughts.)

For all man's efforts and increase in scientific knowledge, since the time of Job, we are no closer to controlling the weather than Job was.

The verbiage used in these verses (Job 38:34-35) is one of a commander giving orders to his troops:

> *For I also am a man under authority, with soldiers under me; and I say to this one, "Go!" and he goes, and to another, "Come!" and he comes, and to my slave, "Do this!" and he does it.*
>
> — Matthew 8:9

The closest we've come to telling lightning where to go is the use of lightning rods.

Plus, Job already knew well who controlled the rain and the thunderbolt:

> *When he gave to the wind its weight and apportioned the waters by measure, when he made a decree for the rain and a way for the lightning of the thunder.*
> —Job 28:25-26

God reminds Job that it is instinctive within mankind (and, may I say, within the animal kingdom as well) to have an understanding and be able to perceive when a storm is approaching.

This is a God-given, created ability through all our natural senses, to sense a change in the weather. Most of us (including myself) don't rely upon our senses and have thus dulled our perception, relying upon the news to forecast tomorrow's weather.

Light, air temperature, moisture, wind direction, and cloud movement all give us clues to what tomorrow may hold. I have even known people who could sense a drop in barometric pressure and use a weather stick to predict storms. Have you ever heard the expression or even said yourself "Smells like rain!" Have you ever heard the saying "Red sky at night sailors delight, Red sky in morning sailors take warning."

> *The Pharisees and Sadducees came up, and testing Jesus, they asked Him to show them a sign from heaven.*
>
> *But He replied to them, "When it is evening, you say , 'It will be fair weather, for the sky is red.' And in*

the morning, 'There will be a storm today, for the sky is red and threatening.' Do you know how to discern the appearance of the sky, but can not discern the signs of the times?"

— Matthew 16:1-3

With all that was happening, Job was beginning to get beat down and frustrated. Then his "friends" stopped by and proceeded to tell him that it was all his fault! But God, through an act of weather, once again reminds Job of who He is.

God reminds Job that even though there is a basic wisdom and instincts within man, they still cannot comprehend the vastness of His work or control the outcome.

"Who has put wisdom in the innermost being or given understanding to the mind? Who can count the clouds by wisdom, or tip the water jars of the heavens, When the dust hardens into a mass And the clods stick together?"

True wisdom belongs to God and is shared according to His will!

To me, the interesting point of this conversation is that it takes place DURING THE TEMPEST OR STORM. It's almost like God was giving a practical demonstration of rain and lightning and saying, "Oh, by the way, Job, can you do this?!"

So, no matter what is in our life's forecast, we can count on the fact that all the rain and lightning is happening exactly where and when it is supposed to, and we need to keep our senses keenly tuned by reading His Word. We need to listen to the Holy Spirit and our God- given conscience in order to have an understanding of what is happening around us and weather the storms.

> *Is it not the wheat harvest today? I will call to the LORD, that He may send thunder and rain. Then you will know and see that your wickedness is great which you have done in the sight of the LORD by asking for yourselves a king.*
> — 1 Samuel 12:17

* Zecariah 10:1, Jeremiah 14:22, Amos 5:8

CHAPTER 18:

"Anything You Have Done, I Have Done Better"

Can you hunt the prey for the lion, or (can you) satisfy the appetite of the young lions, when they crouch in their dens and lie in wait in their lair? Who prepares for the raven its nourishment, when its young cry to God and wander about without food?

— Job 38:39-41

As we finish with Chapter 38, God gets into one of my favorite parts of this conversation with Job.

Here God starts to have Job review the animal kingdom. After all, God did create them on the same day as man, and gave man dominion over them. God even had Adam name them all.

Once again, God goes to extreme opposites to make His point.

Before all these disasters fell upon him, Job was not only known as a righteous man, but also a very generous man as well.

In earlier chapters, Job mentions his generosity. Not only was he defending his character, but I'm sure he was also reminiscing of better days.

Job had wealth, power, and position; he used these wisely. Job was a blessing to all those he came in contact with. Now all that was gone!!!

> *Whoever heard me, spoke well of me, and those who saw me commended me, because I rescued the poor who cried for help, and the fatherless who had none to assist them. The one who was dying blessed me; I made the widow's heart sing. I put on righteousness as my clothing; justice was my robe and my turban. I WAS eyes to the blind and feet to the lame. I WAS a father to the needy; I took up the case of the stranger. I broke the fangs of the wicked and snatched the victims from their teeth.*
>
> —Job 29:11-17

> *Have I not wept for those in trouble? Has not my soul grieved for the poor?*
>
> —Job 30:25

> *IF I HAVE DENIED the desires of the poor OR LET the eyes of the widow grow weary, IF I HAVE KEPT my bread to myself, NOT SHARING IT with the fatherless- BUT from my youth I reared them as a father would, and from my birth I guided the widow- IF I have seen ANYONE perishing for lack of clothing, or the needy without garments, and THEIR HEARTS BLESSED ME for warming them with the fleece from my sheep, IF I have raised my hand against the fatherless knowing that I had influence in court, then let my arm fall from the shoulder, let it be broken off at the joint.*
>
> —Job 31:16-22

But now, here at the end of Chapter 38, God presents His character and asks Job to make a comparison.

God asked two very obvious questions. I don't believe He did this to humble Job, since Job would have had the same answer to the questions even BEFORE he lost everything!!

> *Can you hunt the prey for the lion, or (can you) satisfy the appetite of the young lions, when they crouch in their dens and lie in wait in their lair? Who prepares for the raven its nourishment, when its young cry to God and wander about without food?*
>
> —Job 38:39-41

God once again REDIRECTED Job's focus. Job needed to take his eyes off himself and his situation. God was saying, "Job, you remember all the good things you did and were able to do. But, even in your best of times could you do either of these? Anything you could do, I do even better!!"

"Can you hunt the prey for the lion…"

The Lion is the "King of beasts" and "Ruler of the jungle." He has no predators (except man) and is at the top of the food chain. He doesn't need your help.

The lion in both Scripture and other writings is symbolic of several things. Often a ruthless, almost unstoppable killer that works from ambush. A lion's roar is said to be heard for miles and often spreads fear into those that hear it. Lions in the Old Testament evoke ferocity, destructive power, and irresistible strength. They also symbolize a bold and valiant warrior and absolute power.

The lion is the epitome of a proud, self-sufficient ruler!!
Yet, they rely upon God for food.

The lions roar for their prey and seek their food from God.

— Psalm 104:21

When the environment is good and prey is plentiful, there is no need. Lions generally hunt by ambush or stalking up close to their intended prey, often getting within 30 yards before attacking. The home range of a carnivore is generally as large as necessary (may be several hundred square miles) but as small as possible to satisfy energetic needs (as little as 50-60 square miles). (Gittleman and Harvey, 1982; MacDonald, 1983). The upper and lower limits are determined by energy expenditure during territorial defense and food availability respectively (MacDonald, 1983).

> *The old lion perisheth for lack of prey, and the stout lion's whelps are scattered abroad.*
> — Job 4:11 (KJV)

Next, God goes from the "king of beasts" to the symbol of death and destruction, the raven!

> *"Who prepares for the raven its nourishment, when its young cry to God and wander about without food?"*

Ravens are numerous in Palestine. In general appearance, they resemble the crow, but much larger. Ravens are almost two feet long, glossy black, with whiskers around the beak, and rather stiff-pointed neck feathers. Generally thought to be among the most intelligent of birds, they have a brazen disposition. This bird has been an object of interest throughout history. In captivity, they have been able to speak sentences of a few words when carefully taught. The raven's uncanny acts have made it a bird surrounded by superstition, myth, fable, and also connected with the religious rites of many nations.

The raven is a scavenger that relies on finding and feeding on dead (or dying) animals. They have a varied diet and also eat the young of other birds, very small animals, seeds, berries, and fruit. They work in small flocks (actually called an "unkindness of ravens") or family units to survive. They are noisy, with a loud, rough, emphatic cry. Their young are clamorous at feeding time.

In Scripture, ravens are associated with death, owls, and uninhabited ruins. They are also put with those that eat dead carcasses like vultures.

In Genesis, Noah let the raven out first to see if the waters had receded. It flew around and came back to the ark but did not re-enter the ark with Noah and the other animals. Ravens were considered unclean in Leviticus; they were expressions of God's wrath and the unrighteous. Since the time of Noah, it was considered a curse to be eaten by birds.

YET, when God directly speaks of the raven, He uses it as a symbol of His caring for us.

> *He provides food for the cattle and for the young ravens when they call.*
>
> — Psalm 147:9

> *Consider the ravens[13]: for they neither sow nor reap; which neither have storehouse nor barn; and God feedeth them: how much more are ye better than the fowls?*
>
> — Luke 12:24

EVERYBODY is dependent on God, from the very wealthy, powerful and self-sufficient, to the poor and needy. This is a good place for us to put our own situation into perspective.

13 *Korax* = the Greek word for raven, which occurs only once in one verse in the Greek concordance.

CHAPTER 19:

"You've Got to Be Kiddin' Me!!" *or* "Timing Is Everything!!"

There is an appointed time for everything. And there is a time for every event under heaven — A time to give birth and a time to die...

— Ecclesiastes 3:1-2

In the next verses (or really the next few chapters!) God moves us to the fifth and sixth day of His work. He continues to direct Job (and us) to look outside ourselves and what we think that we understand.

God gently has us look around, in the face of ALL THAT WE DO KNOW, and see how much MORE WE DON'T KNOW.

As He does this, He redirects us and has us look at the very source of all knowledge — HIM.

> *Do you know the time the mountain goats give birth? Do you observe the calving of the deer? Can you count the months they fulfill, Or do you know the time they give birth? They kneel down, they bring forth their young, They get rid of their labor pains. Their offspring become strong, they grow up in the open field; They leave and do not return to them.*
>
> — Job 39:1-4

Speaking as a father of three and a grandfather of three, there is nothing like the miracle of birth (although it technically doesn't meet the definition of a miracle).

Job was a father, and I'm sure he shared those anxious moments along with his wife. Waiting in anticipation for the birth of each of their children.

We've come a long way since the days of Job. Doctors are now able to tell not only the sex of the child, but a vast array of other important information, even before the baby is born!!

But, what about that all important due date? Did you know that most doctors are trying to get away from that terminology? Instead they are leaning towards "ESTIMATED day of arrival."

Rather than assigning an actual delivery date, they are estimating a day of arrival in order to help the doctors determine other milestones in pregnancy. According to information from the Prenatal Institute, a non-profit organization, data shows that an estimated date of delivery is rarely accurate, reporting only about 4% of babies are actually born on their due date!!

> *"Do you know the time the mountain goats give birth?"*

Job could, quite conceivably, know some facts of nature from simple observation. Yet even this relatively low level of knowledge was beyond him.

This "mountain goat" was most likely the Nubian ibex, sometimes called the rock goat or wild goat. This goat is a desert-dwelling species found in the mountainous areas of Algeria, Israel, Jordan, Saudi Arabia, Oman, Egypt, Ethiopia, Eritrea, Yemen, Lebanon, and the Sudan. It resembles the common goat but is larger. Females can weigh 65 pounds and large males can weigh over 200 pounds. Both males and females have horns that are much longer than an average goat (sometimes considerably more than a yard in length).

The ibex live on rocky ledges and cliffs where most animals would fear to go! It's both frightening and exciting to see them jump from one rock to another or walk along a narrow rocky ledge. It's awe inspiring to watch their assent and descent on sheer vertical cliffs!! But God has given this goat just the kind of feet needed.

The Nubian has a small hoof, something like those of a sheep. The difference is that it is hollow underneath, with a ridge around it. This design enables the animal can cling to the rock (like a cleat) and keep from slipping.

The Nubian ibex also has a special way to deal with the hot, dry climates of the African and Arabian mountains: their shiny coats reflect sunlight and keep them cool.

Nubian ibex males use scent to communicate with potential mates. The males use their beards to spread a scent that draws in and excites females during breeding season (the rut).

Once pregnant, the female will have a gestation period of 147 to 180 days. She will give birth to anywhere from one to three kids. Female Nubians give birth to their young at the end of the dry season, high up on steep mountainous ledges.

Right after birth, a kid is very alert and can jump around. At four weeks, it is ready to join the other kids in the group. At four to six months, a kid is weaned, but will remain with its mother for at least a year.

Yet, with all that we now know about the Ibex, I have not found a single hint of even one having been seen giving birth in the wild. All said and done, even as doctors with all their information can only give an "estimated day of arrival" for human infants, no one but God "knows the time when the mountain goat gives birth."

> "Do you observe the calving of the deer? Can you count the months they fulfill, Or do you know the time they give birth?"

The word "ayahal" for deer used here most often refers to the roe deer. (The English has sometimes been rendered "hart" and "hind," which in turn often refers to the red deer. Yet, the red deer does not inhabit the area of Syria or Palestine.) The roe deer inhabits not only Great Britain and Europe, but commonly as far south as Palestine. The word occurs in the Bible 22 times, while "yachmur" occurs only twice (in the list of clean animals in Deuteronomy 14:5, and in 1 Kings 4:23, in the list of animals provided for Solomon's table). In both places the King James Version has "fallow deer" and the Revised Version (British and American) "roebuck." In view of the fact that the roe deer have been and are common in Palestine, while the occurrence of the fallow deer is doubtful, it seems reasonable to render "ayahal" — "roe deer" or "roebuck."

The polygamous roe deer males clash over territory in early summer and mate in early autumn. During courtship, when the males chase the females, they often flatten the underbrush, leaving behind areas of the forest in the shape of a figure eight called roe rings. Males may also use their antlers to shovel fallen foliage and soil around as a way of attracting a mate. Roebucks enter rutting during the July and August breeding season.

Females are monoestrous, meaning they breed only once a year. (Humans have a menstrual cycle in place of an estrous cycle). Generally speaking, the timing of estrus is coordinated with seasonal availability of food and other circumstances such as migration or predation. This design ends up maximizing the offspring's chances of survival.

Some species are actually able to modify their estral timing in response to external conditions. Female roe deer can have delayed implantation, called obligate diapause.

The embryo does not immediately implant in the uterus after the doe is bred (creating the zygote), but is maintained in a state of dormancy. Little to no development takes place while the embryo remains unattached to the uterine wall. As a result, the normal gestation period is extended for a species-specific time. (While much of the molecular regulation involved in activating the dormant embryo has been characterized, little is still known about entry into dormant state and the conditions which enable it to remain dormant.)

All this enables the survival of the female roe deer, avoiding risk to their own lives during unfavorable environmental conditions. It also helps time the birth of their offspring for a more favorable metabolic and/or environmental condition.

Roe deer usually give birth to two spotted fawns of opposite sexes. The fawns remain hidden from predators in long grass; they are suckled by their mother several times a day for around three months. Roe deer adults often abandon their young if they sense or smell that another animal or a human has been near it. Young female roe deer can begin to reproduce when they are around six months old.

> *"Their offspring become strong, they grow up in the open field; They leave and do not return to them."*

(A looser translation = They grow up, leave their mother and fend for themselves, all without man's help.)

Though Job probably did not have such detailed knowledge of the Nubian ibex and the roe deer, or these principles of the natural order; he likely had a basic knowledge, just through observation. Either way, Job had to admit that the natural order of these events seemed to work pretty well.

All these questions bring before us another question. A question that we need to ask ourselves "If I can understand:"

1. At the very beginning God gave a simple command to his creation "be fruitful and multiply."
2. God gave His creation unique abilities to carry out that task.
3. If I can see and understand that this world, made by God, operates with remarkable order and wisdom, can I doubt His wisdom and handling of all things in my life just because there are things in my life I can't understand?

God is not just kidding around. He will bring about all He has planned by His scheduled "due date."

> *Trust in the LORD with all your heart and lean not on your own understanding...*
> — Proverbs 3:5 (NIV)

> *To every [thing there is] a season, and a time to every purpose under the heaven...*
> — Ecclesiastes 3:1 (KJV)

CHAPTER 20:

"Who Let the Dogs (Donkeys) Out!!!"

When we think of animals, they often represent various things to us. For example, cheetah = speed, bull = strength, peacock = beauty, dove = peace.

In these next verses, God speaks to Job (and us) about several animals that I'm sure Job was familiar with. Each of these animals represented certain traits that God wanted Job to think about.

As we continue to listen in on God's conversation with His servant Job, we are going to look through Job's eyes at two admired yet unruly animals.

> *Who let the wild donkey go free? Who untied its rope? I gave it the wasteland as its home, the salt flat as its habitat. It laughs at the commotion in the town; it does not hear a driver's shout. It ranges the hills for its pasture and searches for any green thing.*
>
> *Will the wild ox consent to serve you, or will he spend the night at your manger? Can you bind the wild ox in a furrow with ropes, or will he harrow the valleys after you? Will you trust him because his strength is great and leave your labor to him? Will you have faith in him that he will return your grain and gather it from your threshing floor?*
>
> —Job 39: 5-12

For now, we'll look at the wild donkey.

The ass family has two major branches: the African lineage and the Eurasian lineage. But the Asiatic wild ass is truly feral and doesn't appreciate or even tolerate the presence of people. The Asiatic wild ass belongs to the same genus as the domestic horse, is about the same size, and looks much like a horse. (This species is not the ancestor or foundation of our more familiar donkey of today. The African lineage, such as the Somalia wild ass, is the lineage that was domesticated.).

The Eurasian lineage has never been domesticated, and is notoriously untameable. In fact, the Hebrew name for the Asiatic Ass is "pere," which means wild. Its lack of a rigid dominance hierarchy (unwillingness to accept the elaborate system of social cues needed to enforce it) may explain why the Asiatic wild ass cannot be domesticated. (Their social structure is similar to that of Grevy's zebra, which also cannot be domesticated.)

All that being said, God put before Job the wild donkey!

The onager was possibly one of the most admired animals of the Old Testament world. To be labeled a "wild ass" was both a compliment and/or a slight.

- compliment in the enviable freedom and an ability to survive.
- to be slighted or admired — as one who is considered uncontrollable, independent, self-governing, your own boss.[14]

The sharpness of sarcasm is demonstrated in Job 11:12. As Zophar labeled Job a witless, empty-headed man with as much chance to become wise as a wild donkey has to be born tame.

— Elmer Bernard Smick

In our American culture, a more relative symbol would probably be the wild mustang. Beauty, speed, power — FREEDOM.

But, as we look at this free and uncontrollable beast, God steps into our line of sight.

God once again says, "Look at everything around you. Now think about Me!"

> *"Who let the wild donkey go free? Who untied its rope? I gave it the wasteland as its home, the salt flat as its habitat."*

"WHO?" Man was given the ability and position to domesticate animals (Genesis 1:26). It is God who gave the wild donkey its freedom!! BUT God did not free something that man had previously bound!!! The wild donkey was never penned or roped to begin with!! It's laughable that man thinks he can bind or control what God has set free!!!

"I gave." God emphasized that along with that freedom. He was the one who established the wild donkey's dwelling place and how it should live.

In the beginning, Job was focused on God and accepted his situation, yet not without sorrow.

> *He said, "Naked I came from my mother's womb and naked I shall return there. The Lord gave and the Lord has taken away. Blessed be the name of the Lord." Through all this Job did not sin nor did he blame God.*
>
> — Job 1:21-22

> *Then his wife said to him, "Do you still hold fast your integrity? Curse God and die!"*
>
> *But he said to her, "You speak as one of the foolish women speaks. Shall we indeed accept good from God and not accept adversity?" In all this Job did not sin with his lips.*
>
> — Job 2:9-10

But, like many of us, as time goes on and with no relief, faith is tested and stretched. Add to that the attacks and accusations of his "friends"! In an effort to defend himself, Job began to lose that focus. He knew God was not punishing him. (Job 2:3, "GOD says …although you incited Me against him to ruin him without cause.'")

Yet, to defend himself against the accusations of these men, Job was put into a position of either giving a reason for his condition, or being set free from it.

In Chapter 3 Job cursed the day he was born and saw death as a release. Vs. 17-19, "There the wicked cease from raging, and there the weary are at rest. The prisoners are at ease together; They do not hear the voice of the taskmaster. The small and the great are there, and the slave is free from his master."

God is continuing to get Job back in focus. God is the One who is in charge. "I gave" freedom that no man can bind or control.

But, hidden — out in the open — is an understanding that God has also put a cost to this uncontrollable freedom. God has everything in balance, just as in Job 38:15, where God tells Job, "From the wicked their light is withheld, And the uplifted arm is broken."

For those who want this unbridled freedom, to "laugh at the commotion in the town," and "not hear a driver's shout or have to respond to the voice of authority," God says "I give you the wasteland as its home, the salt flat as its habitat" and "To roam the hills for your pasture and search for any green thing."

The word for "wasteland" meant just that! The land was often considered and described as barren, sterile and in some ways uninhabitable. Food and water were hard to come by and the wild donkey was constantly "searching for ANY green thing." (The word gives a picture of the intensity of just trying to survive.)

Job previously used the wild donkey as an example to both rationalize his anguish and express the harshness of his life.

> *Does the wild donkey bray over his grass, Or does the ox low over his fodder?*
>
> *—Job 6:5*

The braying of the wild donkey and the lowing of the ox shows distress and want of palatable food.

> *Behold, as wild donkeys in the wilderness, they go forth seeking food in their activity, as bread for their children in the desert.*
>
> *—Job 24:5*

God heard the braying of Job and reminded him of the Master's hand (See again: Job 1:21-22; Job 2:9-10 "Shall we indeed accept good from God and not accept adversity?")

The question is "Are you bound?" If so, to what or to whom?

> *So if the Son makes you free, you will be free indeed.*
>
> *—John 8:36*

> *To hear the groaning of the prisoner, To set free those who were doomed to death…*
>
> *— Psalm 102:20*

For the law of the Spirit of life in Christ Jesus has set you free from the law of sin and of death.
— Romans 8:2

What else can we see about this wild donkey that "laughs at the commotion in the town; it does not hear a driver's shout" and is free to "range(s) the hills for its pasture?"

Wild donkey=freedom=happiness!! We all seek freedom" in one way or another. "Can't wait to grow up and be able to do what I want to do!" "Things would be better if I were my own boss." Both statements are based on a desire to be free of our restrictions and those things that bind us, believing that if we can break those bonds, we would be happier.

If you're not bound, are you free and uncontrollable like the wild donkey? Or are you free to serve?

God presents to Job the bond between the One served and the one who serves. He gives freedom to those uncontrollable and wild things. Yet, He still determines where, and the limits of what they can do.

God had a special relationship with Job. "MY SERVANT JOB" (Job 1:8, 2:3, and 42:7-8, four times)

Act as free men, and do not use your freedom as a covering for evil, but use it as bondslaves of God.
— 1 Peter 2:16

So, the next time that urge to be free from your present situation strikes, stop and recognize WHO it is that gives true freedom, and listen for the "driver's shout."

For even when we were with you, we used to give you this order: if anyone is not willing to work, then he is not to eat, either.

— 2 Thessalonians 3:10

An ox knows its owner, and a donkey its master's manger, But Israel does not know, My people do not understand.

— Isaiah 1:3

....

14 Ishmael in Genesis 16:12 / Job 11:12

CHAPTER 21:

"As Strong as an Ox" *or* "Do You Trust Me?"

Last time I stated there were two animals which were highly regarded back in Old Testament times. We took a quick look at the wild donkey.

This time I want to get an idea of what God was presenting to Job, in the image of the wild ox.

> Will the wild ox consent to serve you, or will he spend a night at your manger? Can you bind the wild ox in a furrow with ropes, or will he harrow the valleys after you? Will you trust him because his strength

is great and leave your labor to him? Will you have faith in him that he will return your grain, and gather it from your threshing floor?

— Job 39:9-12

The word used here is "re'em" (pronounced "reh-am") and most likely refers to the great aurochs or wild bull, which is now extinct. The exact meaning is not known.

"Unicorn" occurs in the King James Version (the King James Version margin "rhinoceros"), while the Revised Version (British and American) has "wild-ox" everywhere (margin "ox-antelope"). The Septuagint has monokeros ("one-horned"[15])except in Isaiah 34:7, where we find hoi hadroi, "the large ones," "the bulky ones."

As much as I am a word person, in this case I have to lean towards the context for a better understanding of the animal presented here. Still giving what I believe to be a possible, though unlikely, explanation for the second meaning.

This massive animal, now extinct, was the wild species from which domesticated cattle have been derived. It was larger than most modern breeds and the bulls had long horns pointing forward and upward.

In early times the aurochs ranged over much of Europe, Western and Central Asia, and parts of North Africa, including Egypt. There are historic records of Thotmosis III (c. 1500 BC), that say he traveled far to hunt one. The last Egyptian documented evidence dates back to around 1190 BC (Rameses III).

Assyrian kings also hunted it heavily, but it survived in the less inhabited parts of Mesopotamia until a few centuries ago. The last recorded European specimen died in 1627 AD.

The contexts of several occurrences provide some useful information:

- Numbers 23:22 and Numbers 24:8 NIV, "… the strength of a wild ox." — The auroch was one of the largest and most powerful wild ungulates known.
- Deuteronomy 33:17 speaks of the horns and having a majesty with decisive power.

These passages imply a close acquaintance with the animal and leave little doubt in my mind that the wild ox is being described. It was a familiar member of the fauna of nearby lands.

The mentioning of this animal in Job 39 and relating it to local agriculture practices strongly suggests to me that it was more closely related to our oxen of today.

So, why would God bring up a "dumb ox?" Why would this animal be so significant in Job's eye?

As cultures change or "advance," our dependence on various things changes. It would be difficult to imagine our lives today without the inventions of the railroad, the automobile, the truck, the airplane, computers and cell phones. Our very economy as a nation depends upon the use of such items.

In our modern and mechanized society, it's hard for us to get a picture of exactly what is being presented here.

There was no animal in the rural economy that was held in higher esteem than the ox, and deservedly so! All the ordinary operations of farming and the general economy depended upon the ox! Oxen were used for ploughing, for treading out corn, for draught purposes. They were generally yoked in pairs, as beasts of burden. They were used for meat and used in the sacrifices. Cows supplied milk and butter.

Connected with the importance of oxen in the rural economy of the Jews, there were strict code of laws (mercifully set forth by God) for their protection and preservation.

- The ox that threshed the corn was by no means to be muzzled (Deuteronomy 25:4).
- The ox was to enjoy rest on the Sabbath as well as his master (Exodus 23:12).
- For other commandments concerning ox see: Exodus 21:28-36; Exodus 22:1-10.
- Exodus 23:4 CSB says, "If you come across your enemy's stray ox or donkey, you must return it to him."
- Deuteronomy 22: 1-10;
- Deuteronomy 5:21 CSB, "Do not covet your neighbor's wife or desire your neighbor's house, his field, his male or female slave, his ox or donkey, or anything that belongs to your neighbor."

To make a long story short, the ox was a symbol of strength, provision, and economic security. A man that had an ox was doing comfortably (probably what we would call middle class).

A man that had a "yoke of oxen was well off (probably upper middle class). Someone owning more than a single yoke of oxen was wealthy.

According to Job 1:3, Job's estate (before he lost everything) included seven thousand sheep and goats, three thousand camels, five hundred yoke of oxen, five hundred female donkeys, and a very large number of servants. Job was the greatest man among all the people of the east.

(* Just as a side note here: Often, we fall into the temptation of seeing the very wealthy as corrupt or arrogant, and yes, there are those that fall into that category. But, having wealth is not the sin. Job was considered by God to be among the most righteous of men!)

As we look at this ox, God refocused Job on the source of the "security of his provision."

This massive and powerful wild ox that could NOT be bound and forced into labor; NOR would it sleep contently in a stable.

> *"Will the wild ox consent to serve you, or will he spend a night at your manger? Can you bind the Wild ox in a furrow with ropes, or will he harrow the valleys after you?"*

Even if one were able to use this animal as labor, utilizing its tremendous size and power, the wild ox would be nothing more than a tool.

This tremendous beast, in and of itself, could not accomplish the tasks needed without the supervision of the master's hand.

> *"Will you trust him because his strength is great and leave you labor to him? Will you have faith in him that he will return your grain, and gather it from your threshing floor?"*

God was reminding Job that He is the same God that he knew before all these things happened.

In the wild donkey, God had Job thinking about the "WHO" that is the source of true freedom, the One who sets the course of our lives.

Here in the wild ox, God reminds us that we are to put our trust and faith in Him alone! He is the One who gives us our stability and meets our needs.

Right now, have you or will you TRUST HIM (God) because of who He is, and leave your labors, your cares and your worries to Him?

Will you have FAITH IN HIM (God) that He will provide for your every need from the very start to the finish, from the field to the threshing floor?

(By the way... oxen are smart. The expression "dumb as an ox" couldn't be further from the truth. Oxen are as least as smart as dogs. They can remember individual people and places.)

---

15 For those that hold and translate the word as "unicorn" or "one-horned" there has been archeologic evidence showing the existence of several one-horned animals existing at some point in history. None of this evidence occurs in the area where Job is believed to have been from nor do any completely fill the context in which the word is used.

CHAPTER 22:

"That Just Doesn't Make Any Sense" *or* "Batteries Not Included" *or* "You Are Who I Say You Are"

How many of you have ever had one of those days when nothing made any sense? I know I've had my fair share. This is exactly where Job was. Nothing was making any sense.

In these next several verses, God has His servant Job think about a fourth animal, the ostrich.

Unlike the other animals mentioned before, this member of the animal kingdom is NOT very highly thought of! The ostrich is often associated with desolation and the unwelcome.

> *I go about mourning without comfort; I stand up in the assembly and cry out for help. I have become a brother to jackals and a companion of ostriches.*
> — Job 30:28-29

But, just as with the previous examples, God has a very positive and important point to make.

Let's join Job as God speaks to him about this unusual bird, and what it says to us.

Contemporary ostriches are native to Africa. All living ostriches are considered to be members of a single species, Struthio Camelus. Presently there are more than ten extinct species described from Africa and Asia.

As noted in Chapter 30, Job made reference to the bird, so it was familiar to him.

As the largest and fastest flightless birds around, ostriches are one of the most recognizable bird species in the world (some can weigh up to 300 lbs. and stand more than 6 ft. tall). But their physical stature isn't the only interesting thing about these birds — their reproductive behavior is also peculiar and sets them apart.

> *The wings of the ostrich wave proudly, but are they the pinions and plumage of love? For she leaves her*

eggs to the earth and lets them be warmed on the ground, forgetting that a foot may crush them and that the wild beast may trample them. She deals cruelly with her young, as if they were not hers; though her labor be in vain, yet she has no fear, because God has made her forget wisdom and given her no share in understanding. When she rouses herself to flee, she laughs at the horse and his rider.

— Job 39:13-18

Here God points out some positives and what sounds like an apparent "flaw" or "negative" trait in the ostrich.

Something is missing! But why? How is this information supposed to be either an admonishment or encouragement to Job? How is God revealing anything about Himself with this information? Let's look at the three areas God mentioned about this unique bird:

- its elaborate plumage and mating ritual ("but not the plumage of love")
- its rather disappointing "parenting style"
- the bird's blinding speed

The first point of interest —

"The wings of the ostrich wave proudly, but are they the pinions and plumage of love?" (NASB)[16]

I believe a more direct translation and a close examination of the ostrich's nature can help us gain a possible understanding of what God was trying to point out.

Let's take a look at this very unusual flightless bird and hopefully see what God reveals to us.

The ostrich, like many other birds, has a very elaborate mating ritual. Male ostriches undergo a skin color change at breeding season. His skin turns bright red. This involuntary color change lets the hens know that he's ready to mate!! The male attracts as many hens as possible by dancing, fluffing his feathers, flapping his wings with an alternating wing beat, and swinging his head around. Along with this elaborate dance, he will make loud, hollow-sounding booms to attract hens. The loudest voice and the fanciest dancing technique makes him a successful breeder and attracts more females to his harem.

The female ostrich who is won over by his displays will hold her wings out from her sides, shaking the tips. She bobs her head up and down while holding it low to the ground. At the same time, she opens and closes her beak. She then crouches, telling the male she's ready. He approaches her with a rapid footwork dance and then mounts her and crouches with one foot on the ground and the other on her back. While mating, the male groans and the female snaps her beak and shakes her head.

In a single season, males will mate with multiple females. (This fact is important when we examine God's second point.)

Unquestionably, the mating ritual of the ostrich is exciting, and most likely a very splendid thing to observe. But is it really all what it seems to be? Does this reveal the whole story? Does all this outward flamboyant display translate into the perfect love story?

> *"The wings of the ostrich wave proudly… BUT…"*

…second point of interest:

> *"For she leaves her eggs to the earth and lets them be warmed on the ground, forgetting that a foot may crush them and that the wild beast may trample them. She deals cruelly with her young, as if they were not hers; though her labor be in vain, yet she has no fear, because God has made her forget wisdom and given her no share in understanding."*
>
> — Job 39:14-17

God is a little more explicit in pointing out this facet of the ostrich and thus draws some attention. This just doesn't seem natural and right.

Remember, God is talking to Job at a time of need!! What Job needed was to hear from a real friend! Job was questioning "Why?"

The only reason given to Job by his "friends" (and possibly the only one Job himself could think of) was that he had done something terribly wrong! But Job knew that this wasn't the case, and thus defended himself against such accusations. None of what was happening was making any sense to Job! He had been hoping to hear from his God, to plead his case and just get an answer to his question!! (Any of us who has ever asked God "why" have no right to point a finger at Job!)

God was not going to waste this opportunity to both teach and comfort His faithful servant Job.

As usual, those critical of the Bible jump all over the apparent harsh and unfair description the ostrich. Critics try to point out how uneducated or ill-informed the writers of the Old Testament were.

These critics seek to discredit the accuracy and inspiration of Scripture, while defending the ostrich from this unfair character assassination.

The Reader's Digest Association has published numerous books over the years illustrated with many wonderful aspects of nature. One of them is *Marvels and Mysteries of Our Animal World*. Most of these emphasize Darwinian evolutionism. Among those articles there was a comment regarding the ostrich, by Jan Juta (one of the Digest writers):

> *In Chapter 39 of the Book of Job, we find an unflattering reference to the ostrich: "She is hardened against her young ones, as though they were not hers. Because God has deprived her of wisdom, neither hath he imparted to her understanding." Job obviously had never studied the ostrich. Actually the birds are good parents (129).*

As Christians, we need to avoid excusing away what Scripture says every time there seems to be an apparent conflict between God's Word and modern science.

We shouldn't just jump on the bandwagon and say, "Oh, that's just figurative." (Granted, there are many times in Scripture when things are meant to be figurative.) Rather, as with all

Scripture, we need to go to the Author and see if there are any other possible explanations.

In reality, these "well educated critics" are not criticizing the writers of the Old Testament! Scripture is "inspired" (or God-breathed), and therefore, they are criticizing God's description of the ostrich.

That being said, it is our obligation to understand what God is saying and see it through Job's eyes, as it relates to scientific research. We can then make our own judgements and see if Jan Juta of Reader's Digest was correct in her assessment of the ostrich as a "good parent."

As mentioned before, the ostrich has what is called a "polygynous mating type." This is where one male will mate with anywhere between three and seven females. This fact itself is not unusual in the animal kingdom and is not noteworthy.

To this information, add the fact that all these females will share a common ground nest (called a dump nest, prepared by the male). This communal nest can be nearly ten feet across and is simply a shallow hollow formed in the ground.

Each hen lays between two and eleven eggs. After all the egg laying is complete, there can be ten to forty eggs OR MORE!!! (The most ever recorded was seventy-eight!!)

Here is where the problem appears. Due to the size of the eggs, only about twenty eggs can actually be incubated. (Ostrich eggs are six inches in diameter and can weigh up to three pounds.)

As in most of nature, there is an inherent and often competitive drive to reproduce. This is also true of the ostrich. The dominant hen will reject any surplus eggs by pushing them out of the nest. She always ensures, however, that her own eggs remain.

Both the male and the dominant female take turns incubating the nest. (The incubation period is 35 to 45 days.) The dull gray female sits during the day and the black male at night. There are also times when the adult birds will leave the nest, covering the eggs with a layer of dirt (to the depth of about a foot). The habit of the ostrich leaving its eggs to be matured by the sun's heat is usually appealed to in order to confirm the scriptural account:

> *For she abandons her eggs to the earth, and warms them in the dust, she forgets that a foot may crush them or that a wild beast may steal them.*

I believe this is only part of the explanation.

The second part of the picture is the eggs that are left uncovered and kicked to the side. These eggs are completely neglected, not only by the dominant brooding parents, but by the females that lay them in the first place!! Remember, these birds are polygynous!!

On average, this leaves anywhere from 50 to 85% of the females in the group having nothing to do with the eggs. It also means that anywhere from 10 to over 50% of the eggs laid are completely abandoned altogether by all the adult ostriches.

Some Arabic scientific observers write, "The outer layer of eggs is generally so ill covered that they are destroyed in quantities by jackals, wild-cats, etc., and that the natives carry them away, only taking care not to leave the marks of their footsteps, since, when the ostrich comes and finds that her nest is discovered, she crushes the whole brood, and builds a nest elsewhere."

> *She deals cruelly with her young, as if they were not hers; though her labor be in vain, yet she is without concern, because God has made her forget wisdom and given her no share in understanding.*

Ostrich chicks are one of the largest of bird babies and are precocial (meaning they are born covered with feathers, eyes open, and ready to move).

The male ostrich is the main care giver. It is the male ostrich that shows the chicks how to feed and protects them from predators and the elements.

The young ostriches fledge at four to five months and are fully grown by about 18 months, reaching sexual maturity after two to four years.

Fewer than 10% of nests survive the nine-week period of laying and incubation. Of the chicks that survive, only 15% make it the first 18 months.

Biologists have also observed another interesting trait. Since there is strength in numbers, when two ostrich families meet, there will sometimes be a competition for the chicks. In other words, one pair will attempt to drive off the second pair; the losers of the conflict give up their chicks to the victor. Sometimes during a takeover, the adults have also been known to accidentally run over their own young!

Under certain environmental conditions, the family group may break up when chicks are a few weeks old; the adults renew sexual activity and become highly aggressive towards all juveniles. "Chicks fledged in small numbers outside the breeding season are frequently treated as outcasts and live solitarily."

So let's recap this information:

- a majority of the females laying eggs in this dump nest have nothing to do with the eggs or the chicks (50 to 85%).
- numerous eggs that were laid are kicked to the side and never taken care of (10 to 50%).
- Of the eggs that hatch and the chicks that survive, it is the male ostrich that takes care of the young.
- Chicks can be taken over by a more dominant pair.
- Chicks born outside of the normal breeding season are often abandoned.

This leads me to believe that the Scriptures' description, the book of Job, is an accurate depiction of the ostrich's behavior!!

God gives the explanation of this seemingly callous behavior: the batteries are missing!!

It is not a willful disregard for the young and it's NOT A DESIGN FLAW!! God says, "I purposely left something out!!!"

> *Because God has made her forget wisdom, And has not given her a share of understanding.*
>
> —Job 39:17

These two words, wisdom and understanding, are used in a way as to state that something (or someone) has a skill and the ability to perceive a situation and act on it!!

What God is saying here is HE PURPOSELY LEFT THAT OUT!! He didn't say "OOOPPPS!!I forgot something!!" Instead He says, "I made her" and "has not given."

God then quickly brings us to His third point:

> *When she lifts herself on high, She laughs at the horse and his rider.*
> —Job 39:18

The ostrich is the tallest and heaviest species of all living birds. Its bulky body means that flying is out of the question. Yet, God has given it something else.

On the ground, this flightless bird has impressive agility: the ostrich is a superb runner. With an impressive 12-foot stride, this bird has the ability to cover five yards in a single stride when running. The mechanics of running are the same regardless of whether man, beast, or bird. The longer, faster, and more powerful the stride, the faster you go!

Running on its toes (the backward-looking knees are actually more like ankles), the ostrich has unique and large leg muscles up close to the body. Mechanically, this allows the animal to swing its legs more quickly. The long lower leg and lever action it provides makes for a quick and powerful stroke with every stride. (The stronger the force exerted on the ground for the quickest amount of time = acceleration.)

The ostrich can sprint at speeds of up to 45 mph. If pushed (like being chased by a predator or a man on a horse, for example), it can reach a peak speed of 60 mph during short periods. With the ability to accelerate up to 60 mph in approximately two seconds (the 2020 Chevrolet Corvette Stingray Z51 does 0-60 mph in 2.8 seconds) this makes the ostrich the fastest animal on two legs.

The ostrich is also an endurance runner and can jog at 30 mph for as long as half an hour.

Another design advantage is that the ostrich is perfectly proportioned, as the center of gravity is between the long legs and wings. So whatever speed it runs and however much it appears to be out of control, it is always perfectly balanced. When humans run, our leg muscles propel us forward. However, our leg muscles use up lots of energy in keeping us straight. Ostriches have an incredibly efficient approach. They can use all their muscle power to move forward because their center of gravity keeps them perfectly balanced. (Who designed this marvelous animal?)

So what are some of the things we (Job) are supposed to see and learn from God pointing out this marvelous creature to us?

My idea of God speaking:

> *"Job, I know exactly who you are. I know your strengths and your weaknesses. I know because I made you exactly the way I wanted you. No mistakes, no forgetting something, no accidents. I did not set you up for failure, but to survive.*
>
> *"I have set you up to survive and be a testimony to those that put their trust in Me, for generations to come."*

> *We count those blessed who endured. You have heard of the endurance of Job and have seen the outcome of the Lord's dealings, that the Lord is full of compassion and is merciful.*
> — James 5:11

God has designed everything and everyone just the way He wants. And it ALL WORKS.

All our good, all our apparent shortfalls and all our strengths are by HIS Design. We all have our strengths and our weaknesses. He knows what they are. He made us the way we are.

When I was a young Christian, I was told: "Your strengths will always be your strengths And your weaknesses will always be your weaknesses. So work on BOTH."

What are your strengths? What are your weaknesses? Whatever they are, you are who you are by God's design. We need to trust in Him — He will enable us to make it to the end.

> *I can do all this through him who gives me strength.*
> — Philippians 4:13 NIV

(I also want to make it understood that I do not believe God is finished with us! Scripture makes it clear that once we accept Jesus as Lord and are born again, we become "new creatures." We are told to be "transformed." God has also promised that "He who began a good work in you will bring it to completion in the day of Jesus Christ" (Philippians 1:6).

16 This verse has been rendered several different ways by Bible translators. I believe this has been done for the purpose of getting across the "symbolism" of the passage, which is important. The "stork" in the Middle East was known for its beauty and was a symbol of love.

CHAPTER 23:
"Remember the Source of Your Strength" *or* "I'm Not Horsing Around"

Have you ever had one of those tough times when you've had to just dig deep!? We've all heard the stories or watched movies where the main character or hero was at the end of his strength. What about the athlete fighting for that last bit of strength and endurance to come out on top? It's a familiar story, with everyone cheering them on. "Dig deep!" "You can do this!" "Find that inner strength!"

Here in Job 39:19-25, God moves on to the horse and takes a different approach to the problem.

> *Do you give the horse his might? Do you clothe his neck with a mane? Do you make him leap like the locust? His majestic snorting is terrifying. He paws in the valley and exults in his strength; he goes out to meet the weapons. He laughs at fear and is not dismayed; he does not turn back from the sword. Upon him rattle the quiver, the flashing spear, and the javelin. With fierceness and rage he swallows the ground; he cannot stand still at the sound of the trumpet. When the trumpet sounds, he says "Aha!" He smells the battle from afar, the thunder of the captains, and the shouting.*

At first glance, this may not seem unusual. Almost everyone is familiar with horses or has at least seen them. Horses are not exotic and have been domesticated for thousands of years.

Early on, here in the U.S., horses were used for transportation and agriculture. With the onset of mechanization, that purpose was drastically reduced. Currently 30% or less of all horses in the United States are owned for work. Today, most horses are owned for pleasure. In 2020, it was estimated that over 55% of horses in the U.S. were privately owned for pleasure.

So, in order for us to fully understand what God is trying to get across to Job, we need to adjust our thinking.

Back in the time of Job, people just didn't own horses!! Job himself was a very wealthy and influential man, but horses were not listed among his many assets (before Job 1:3; after Job 42:12).

Horses were owned by kings and the very powerful. Their main (and almost sole purpose) was for war! They were symbols of power, authority, and war.

This description of the war-horse helps explain the character given of presumptuous sinners.

> *I have listened and heard, they have spoken what is not right; no man repented of his wickedness, saying, "What have I done?" Everyone turned to his course, like a horse charging into the battle.*
> — Jeremiah 8:6

A man's heart that is set to do evil, is carried by the inordinate appetites and passions of a wicked way.

At this point, a person like this is no longer afraid of the wrath of God and the fatal consequences of his actions.

> *Be not like a horse or a mule, without understanding, which must be curbed with bit and bridle, or it will not stay near you.*
> — Psalm 32:9 ESV

> *The war horse is a false hope for salvation, and by its great might it cannot rescue.*
>
> — Psalm 33:17 ESV

THIS is the picture God is presenting Job. Job was in the midst of a war.

When trials (or tests) come into our lives, Satan wants us to fail. Satan wants us to operate on our own strength. Satan tells us, "You can do this. Dig deep — find your inner strength, that instinct to survive." Satan doesn't mind if *you* fight him — as long as you do it in your own strength.

Picture Job's trials. Satan made the statements to God:

> *But now stretch out your hand and strike everything he has, and he will surely curse you to your face.*
>
> — Job 1:11

> *But now stretch out your hand and strike his flesh and bones, and he will surely curse you to your face.*
>
> — Job 2:5

From the beginning, Satan used those around Job to turn this whole series of events into a fight, a fight between Job and God!

Job's wife said, "Curse God and die." (In other words, "God has turned against you. You can't win. Quit!")

Job rejected that thought.

Satan then uses Job's three "friends" to up the ante: "Job, you've sinned and done something terrible — repent, God is judging you!"

(Obviously this is a lie because God Himself said, "The LORD said to Satan, 'Have you considered My servant Job? For there is no one like him on the earth, a blameless and upright man fearing God and turning away from evil. And he still holds fast his integrity, although you incited Me against him to ruin him without cause.'")

Job was in the fight of his life, and it was wearing on him. His defense was beginning to turn inward.

In chapters 27-31, Job gives his final defense. He systematically presented his integrity and requested that God give an account for His actions!

> *Far be it from me that I should declare you right; Till I die I will not put away my integrity from me. I hold fast my righteousness and will not let it go. My heart does not reproach any of my days.*
>
> —Job 27:5-6

> *I cry out to you, God, but you do not answer; I stand up, but you merely look at me. You turn on me ruthlessly; with the might of your hand you attack me. You snatch me up and drive me before the wind; you toss me about in the storm. I know you will bring me down to death, to the place appointed for all the living. Surely no one lays a hand on a broken man when he cries for help in his distress.*
>
> —Job 30:20-24

> *Oh, that I had one to hear me! Here is my signature! Let the Almighty answer me! Oh, that I had the*

> *indictment written by my adversary! Surely I would carry it on my shoulder; I would bind it on me as a crown; I would give him an account of all my steps; like a prince I would approach him.*
>
> — Job 31:35-37

God had to snap Job back from where he was!

God Himself called Job a blameless and upright man! Job didn't know about the conversations with Satan. Job had no idea why God would seemingly turn against him!

God wanted Job to look at the source of his strength, for the battle he was facing.

> *Do you give the horse his might? Do you clothe his neck with a mane? Do you make him leap like the locust?*

God wasn't asking Job these questions in order to find out the answers. I believe Job wouldn't have a problem with answering "no" to any of these questions.

So why ask?

Because it reminded Job of the source of strength needed to fight this war.

- DO YOU give ….? No, God gives….
- DO YOU clothe…? No, God clothes….
- DO YOU make him leap…? No, God does….

I can imagine God saying:

Job, you don't understand what's going on because you can't!

My ways are higher than yours and there are things going on that you don't need to know.

But I've given you enough to survive… you know ME — trust in ME and rise up.

Your strength and your integrity are not enough!

I AM THE SOURCE that will enable you to face that battle head-on!!!

We all need to operate and know how to fight the good fight. We do this with all that God has given us.

> *I have hidden your word in my heart that I might not sin against you.*
> — Psalm 119:11

> *Your word is a lamp for my feet, a light on my path.*
> — Psalm 119:105

We cannot fight the good fight without drawing upon the TRUE SOURCE of our strength.

> *I am the vine; you are the branches. If you remain in me and I in you, you will bear much fruit; apart from me you can do nothing.*
> — John 15:5

So the next time you see a horse, say to yourself,

You are from God, little children, and have overcome them; because greater is He who is in you than he who is in the world.

— 1 John 4:4

CHAPTER 24:

"Free as a Bird" *or* "Out of Your Hands"

Is it by your understanding that the hawk soars, Stretching his wings toward the south? Is it at your command that the eagle mounts up And makes his nest on high? On the cliff he dwells and lodges, Upon the rocky crag, an inaccessible place. From there he spies out food; his eyes see it from afar. His young ones also suck up blood; And where the slain are, there is he.
— Job 39: 26-30

Some of you may have heard the phrases: "Believe that life is worth living and your belief will help create the fact" (William James) and "You are not the victim of the world, but rather the master of your own destiny. It is your choices and decisions that determine your destiny." (Roy T. Bennett)

The concept that we are in control and there is power in positive thinking still flows through a lot of teaching and counseling today. The concept that we have the ability to direct the outcome of certain events in our lives.

This lie has been with us since the beginning.

> *For God knows that in the day you eat from it your eyes will be opened, and you will be like God, knowing good and evil.*
>
> — Genesis 3:5

Here, towards the end of Chapter 39, God brings up two more animals, each of which were "free as a bird."

God has Job look at the hawk and the eagle.

(In later references within the Bible, these birds are considered unclean. They are often used to denote God's judgement as well as God's saving grace.)

In verses 26-30, God asks Job two very self-reflective questions. I'm sure, once again, Job (or myself for that matter) didn't have to think twice about the answers.

Let's take a look at a couple of things God wanted Job to remember:

> *"Is it by your understanding that the hawk soars, Stretching his wings toward the south?"*

I'm always amazed at how God answers the seemingly complex situations in our lives with the very simple and obvious.

> *"Job (Neal), do you determine how and when the hawk migrates south?"*

This probably would have been a very familiar situation to Job. You see, one of the largest (if not the largest) migrations of raptors in the world occurs over Israel!

Raptors, or birds of prey, can be divided into two different styles of flight: A) Those that flap their wings continually and are able to migrate over water and/or land. B) Those that soar. These birds depend upon thermal currents. Therefore, they fly mainly over land.

The Mediterranean Sea creates bottlenecks in the migration patterns for birds migrating south from Europe. One of these bottlenecks passes right over Israel and Egypt. This has created one of the largest raptor migration paths in the world. Literally millions of birds use these routes to travel between their summer and winter habitats.

During these raptor migrations, thousands of birds can fill the skies between migration zones. (Sometimes this could be just one species.) Birders come from all over to visit two main sites in Israel (one in the north country and the other in the south) in order to view this spectacle of nature.

I can only imagine Job envisioning one of these awe-inspiring migrations and being asked, "Hey Job, did you do this?! How did you ever come up with this!?"

God then brings up another big raptor, the eagle.

(The rare and impressive imperial eagle has often been recorded during these migration flights.)

> "Is it at your command that the eagle mounts up And makes his nest on high? On the cliff he dwells and lodges, Upon the rocky crag, an inaccessible place. From there he spies out food; his eyes see it from afar. His young ones also suck up blood; And where the slain are, there is he."

It is my opinion that the eagle God was presenting here was what is called the Verreaux's eagle.

Coming in at 2.5-3 feet in size and weighing anywhere from 6.5-12 pounds, this predator is literally death from above. Also known as black eagles, these birds of prey feed mainly on the small hyrax.

They hunt entirely while in flight, swooping down rapidly to surprise their unsuspecting prey. Often hunting in pairs, the eagle also eats birds and other small mammals. The Verreaux's eagle searches out its prey in river gorges, rocky outcrops, hills and mountains. They hunt all the way from sea level to over 13,000 feet.

Verreaux's eagles favor a rugged and extreme habitat; it ranges throughout the mountainous and desert terrain. It is at these impressive elevations that the eagle builds its large nest of sticks and grass on the edges of exposed rocky cliffs. (The largest recorded Verreaux's eagle nest is 13 feet high.)

Breeding occurs at different times throughout the year, depending on the region. After mating the female lays two eggs, three to four days apart.

The first chick hatches in about 44 days. The older eaglet sibling normally kills the younger one. This behavior is known as "obligate cainist" and is common in many raptors. This behavior has been observed in more than 90% of nests. The younger dies from either starvation caused by the older eaglet hogging all the food or direct attack from the older chick. Aggression from the older chick has been noted to occur from the day of hatching and as long as two months or more. Fledging and taking flight normally occurs between three and four months of age.

> *His young ones also suck up blood; And where the slain are, there is he.*

In Matthew 24:28 and Luke 17:37, Christ is speaking to His disciples about the Second Coming and Judgement: "And answering they said to Him, 'Where, Lord?' And He said to them, 'Where the body is, there also the vultures (eagles) will be gathered.'"

> *And I saw an angel standing in the sun; and he cried with a loud voice, saying to all the fowls that fly in the midst of heaven, Come and gather yourselves together unto the supper of the great God; That ye may eat the flesh of kings, and the flesh of captains, and the flesh of*

mighty men, and the flesh of horses, and of them that sit on them, and the flesh of all men, both free and bond, both small and great.
— Revelation 19:17-18

So, what is this all about?!

Basically, God is telling Job (and us) that even if he had an understanding of what was going on, it wouldn't give him (or us) the ability to change the events that are taking place.

Job did not have the authority to command those events that were from above ("On the cliff he dwells and lodges, Upon the rocky crag, an inaccessible place").

God, and God alone, has the understanding and the authority to make things happen! He holds for Himself the final judgement.

So the next time you look skyward and have the privilege of seeing a hawk or an eagle soar, think positive and recognize the One who truly cares for you and has both the understanding and the authority to do something about whatever situation you are facing.

CHAPTER 25:

"That Says It All" *or* "I've Said Too Much Already" *and* "We're Not Finished Yet"

STOP & THINK OBSERVE PROCEED

As we move to Chapter 40, God stops His review of creation. This does not, however, mean we can stop and take a break from what is being said! I can imagine hearing God say: "Okay, Job, we're going to take a quick 15-minute break. I want you to stop and really think about what I've already said. Then, it's back to work."

We've seen in Chapters 38 and 39 God presenting Himself as the ONE.

From the beginning (day one), He was the one Who was and is in control.

He designed it, created it, put boundaries on it, while He continues to maintain and manages it. ("It" meaning everything!)

> *Shall a faultfinder contend with the Almighty? He who argues with God, let him answer it.*
>
> — Job 40:2

I think a very liberal and modern paraphrase would sound like this:

> *"Hey Job, I don't have a problem with you asking 'why,' but when you ask Me to give an account for My decisions; you've gone a little too far.*
>
> *"Now that you've thought about all this, what do you have to say? Tell me what your complaint is again? Can you tell Me what I've gotten wrong?"*

We can never be hasty in our reading of God's Word. Every statement is full of meaning. We need to stop and think about what has just been said!

God doesn't mind being quoted, but there are times when we say something, and it comes back to bite us! This was one of those times for Job, as he had to deal with his previous statements.

> *But I desire to speak to the Almighty and to argue my case with God.*
>
> —Job 13:3

> *Oh, that I had someone to hear me! I sign now my defense — let the Almighty answer me; let my accuser put his indictment in writing. Surely I would wear it on my shoulder, I would put it on like a crown.*
>
> *I would give him an account of my every step; I would present it to him as to a ruler.*
>
> —Job 31:35-37

In Chapter 31, Job is now satisfied with his defense. He has gone from speaking and "reasoning" with God (13:3) to making it a court case. He enters his Not Guilty plea (he has signed the paper.)

It's now up to the prosecution (God) to prove him wrong and bring forth the charges against him. (We all know that it was Satan who brought all this upon Job, but Job was unaware of the conversation that took place in Heaven.)

Now Job had to eat those words! (Trust me, I've had to do that numerous times and it's not very tasty!)

> *Then Job answered the Lord and said, "Behold, I am insignificant; what can I say in response to You? I put my hand on my mouth. I have spoken once, and I will not reply; or twice, and I will add nothing more."*
>
> — Job 40:4-5

The word "insignificant" is translated several different ways, i.e., vile, small account, unworthy, or nothing. No matter which way you read it, in the Hebrew there is no suggestion of moral failure.

Quite literally it means, "of no weight." Job is not confessing moral failure, but a comparative insignificance. ("The fear of God is the beginning of wisdom.")

The act of "putting one's hand over his mouth" was a sign of total submission! We (myself included) would do well to follow suit.

> *What man is he that desireth life, and loveth many days, that he may see good? Keep thy tongue from evil, and thy lips from speaking guile.*
>
> — Psalm 34:12-13 Darby

> *For the one who desires life, to love and see good days, must keep his tongue from evil and his lips from speaking deceit.*
>
> — 1 Peter 3:10

These were not the last words of Job, as we will see in Chapter 42, but God had brought Job (and hopefully us) to a point where there are no words or beyond words.

The difference in Job's tone was not because Job's circumstances had substantially changed. He was still in misery and had lost virtually everything. Job's tone changed because his awareness had changed.

Job once felt that God had forsaken him! He had become focused on his affliction and defending his integrity. He lost his awareness of God's presence! God was silent and nowhere to be found!

> *Oh that I knew how to find Him… Behold, I go forward but He is not there, and backward,* <u>but I cannot perceive Him</u>; *When He acts on the left,* <u>I cannot see Him</u>.
>
> — Job 23:3,8-9

> *Oh that I were as in months gone by, As in the days when God watched over me; When His lamp shone over my head, and by His light I walked through darkness; Just as I was in the days of my youth, when the protection of God was over my tent;* <u>when the Almighty was still with me</u>, *and my children were around me.*
>
> — Job 29:2-5

> *He has thrown me into the mire, and I have become like dust and ashes.* <u>I cry out to You for help, but You do not answer me</u>; *I stand up,* <u>and You turn Your attention against me</u>. *You have become cruel to me; with the strength of Your hand You persecute me.*
>
> — Job 30: 19-21

Now, after this encounter, Job better understood that God, though seemingly silent, was always present.

God was proclaiming the vastness of His wisdom and guidance through the world around him; if only Job would take the time to refocus.

Job (_____ - your name here) look at ME!

God brings the lessons of nature presented in Chapters 38 and 39 to a close. Here in Chapters 40 and 41, God brings out the big guns as He proceeds with the lesson.

These next lessons will deal with what's really going on in Job's life: the internal conflict… the testing of his faith! God is not only concerned with Job's physical well-being but also with strengthening Job's character.

I find it interesting that as God starts the next session, He uses the same phrase He started with in the first part of this dialogue.

> *Gird up thy loins now like a man: I will demand of thee, and declare thou unto me.*
>
> — Job 40:7 KJV

Back in the days of Job, both women and men wore long tunics. Around their waist they would wear a belt or a "girdle."

These garments, though comfortable, would often get in the way of going to battle or doing hard labor. So men would lift their tunics and tuck them into their girdles or tie them in a knot to keep them off the ground. This would make it like wearing a pair of shorts and it would be easier to move around.

Why is this phrase important? God wasn't telling Job to get ready for a physical battle but was requiring Job to answer the questions!

God was teaching Job.

LEARNING (especially the kind that changes or transforms your life) = HARD WORK

> *And be not conformed to this world: but be ye transformed by the renewing of your mind, that ye may prove what [is] that good, and acceptable, and perfect, will of God.*
>
> — Romans 12:2 KJV

Many, many times (especially when times are tough) we need to:

- STOP and THINK about who God is.
- OBSERVE the entirety of creation around us!
- Gird up our loins for the hard work ahead of us; then,
- Proceed.

Let's listen in as God once again directs Job to refocus. And let's give some serious thought about what He has revealed and teaches us through His creation.

CHAPTER 26:

"So You Think You're Qualified for the Job" *or* "Let's Take a Good Look at Things"

Before God presents the last two animals in His review of Creation, He has Job do quick reassessment of their relationship.

As a father of three boys (all grown men now, with families) I would sometimes have to remind them of who's the father or who's the parent.

Here in the next few verses, God was reminding Job of that same thing!

> *Will you even put me in the wrong? Will you condemn me that you may be in the right? Have you an arm like God, and can you thunder with a voice like his?*
>
> *Adorn yourself with majesty and dignity; clothe yourself with glory and splendor.*
>
> *Pour out the overflowings of your anger, and look on everyone who is proud and abase him. Look on everyone who is proud and bring him low and tread down the wicked where they stand. Hide them all in the dust together; bind their faces in the world below.*
>
> *Then will I also acknowledge to you that your own right hand can save you."*
>
> — Job 40:8-14

WOW! You can't get much clearer than that!

I can't put words in God's mouth, but it sounds to me like:

> *"Job, you're right in claiming your innocence. BUT are you going to go so far as to make Me the bad guy!?*

Are you going to bring Me low, in order to elevate yourself?

If you want the job of being 'god', you don't have the qualifications!"

It's easy for us to point a finger at Job and say, "Boy, did you ever screw up!" Yet, I also know, that I've stepped across that line myself.

In the previous chapters God rolled out His qualifications and reminded Job of who He is.

In these next two chapters God will have Job examine who *he* is:

- "Have you an arm like God, and can you thunder with a voice like his? Adorn yourself with majesty and dignity; clothe yourself with glory and splendor." *(Job, do you have the physical ability to do all that is necessary? Can you take on and exhibit the authority to command the situation, and bring it under your control?)*
- "Pour out the overflowings of your anger, and look on everyone who is proud and abase him. Look on everyone who is proud and bring him low and tread down the wicked where they stand. Hide them all in the dust together; bind their faces in the world below." *(Job, do you have the position, character, authority, and power to judge and enact judgement upon all that you see?)*
- "Then will I also acknowledge to you that your own right hand can save you." *(Job, if you can*

pass these next two tests, I'll accept your qualifications to do the job.)

Let's see if any of us qualify for the job.

CHAPTER 27:

"Behold"

In the next two chapters God brings out the big guns. He has Job do an assessment of his qualifications!!

I don't believe the two beasts mentioned in Chapters 40 and 41 are alive today. But the message to us is still the same as it was to Job!

Let's listen in and see if we can get a picture of what God has in store.

Job was most likely familiar with the various animals God presented for his review in Chapters 38 and 39.

I don't see God now jumping to some mythical creatures in Chapters 40 and 41. It's perfectly understandable that some of the animals mentioned earlier had become extinct. I propose these next two beasts were also familiar to Job and are also extinct today.

> *Behold, Behemoth, which I made as I made you; he eats grass like an ox. Behold, his strength in his loins, and his power in the muscles of his belly. He makes his tail stiff like a cedar; the sinews of his thighs are knit together. His bones are tubes of bronze, his limbs like bars of iron. He is the first of the works of God; let him who made him bring near his sword!*
>
> *For the mountains yield food for him where all the wild beasts play. Under the lotus plants he lies, in the shelter of the reeds and in the marsh. For his shade the lotus trees cover him; the willows of the brook surround him. Behold, if the river is turbulent he is not frightened; he is confident though Jordan rushes against his mouth. Can one take him by his eyes, or pierce his nose with a snare?"*
>
> — Job 40:15-24

While there are several opinions concerning this animal (Behemoth), as well as the next animal (Leviathan), I want to make a couple of observations here:

- God paused His conversation with Job to give a special introduction to these two animals.

- God spent 33 verses totally covering the numerous animals in Chapters 38 and 39.
- God spent 44 verses covering these two animals in Chapters 40 and 41.

Therefore, I personally believe that if God wanted to take the time to give these unusual animals special attention. I would do well to do likewise!

I believe Scripture gives us several clues to what a behemoth may have been.

Behold, Behemoth, which I made as I made you… He is the first of the works of God…

I find it fascinating that God says, "BEHOLD!" No other animal did God say that about! It was like putting the animal on stage and shining a spotlight on it. The word(s) are meant to draw your attention to a person, place, or action.

If this was some kind of fictional creature, some extinct "prehistoric unknown animal", or some common everyday animal you might see in the wild (or in a zoo), why the dramatic expression? How would Job be able to BEHOLD a mythological creature or a creature that was not familiar to him?

Which I made as you….

Various translations word this differently, but basically they all mean the same. Even though man has a special place in creation, mankind is still a creation of God. Even though Behemoth was a massive creature, it was still a creation of God.

That puts them both equally subject to their common Creator.

The timing and origin of this animal is also noted:

Behold, Behemoth, which I made as I made you…

The wording here gives the impression of "along with" or "at the same time." So we get the picture of Behemoth being created at the very beginning and the same "day" as mankind.

> *And God said, "Let the earth bring forth living creatures according to their kinds — livestock and creeping things and beasts of the earth according to their kinds." And it was so. And God made the beasts of the earth according to their kinds and the livestock according to their kinds, and everything that creeps on the ground according to its kind. And God saw that it was good.*
> — Genesis 1:24-25

> *Now out of the ground the Lord God had formed every beast of the field and every bird of the heavens and brought them to the man to see what he would call them. And whatever the man called every living creature, that was its name. The man gave names to all livestock and to the birds of the heavens and to every beast of the field. But for Adam there was not found a helper fit for him.*
> — Genesis 2:19-20

Scripture states that God created Behemoth along with the other animals on the same day (the 6th) with man!

If Job was able to behold one, then these animals would have had to survive the Flood and Noah's Ark.

Fossils show that even the largest dinosaurs hatched from eggs. Many of these eggs were a little larger than a football! This scientific fact means it was completely possible for Noah and his family to bring with him on the ark a couple of young sauropods (a dinosaur that best matches the description in Job).

Scientists say that the sauropods were by far the largest land animals that ever lived. Complete skeletal remains have been found (2009) with specimens measuring over 82 feet long, 39 feet high, and having an estimated weight of 65 tons!!

Let's look at God's description of this magnificent animal. Then, let's look at science:

- Scripture: "Behold, his strength in his loins, and his power in the muscles of his belly. He makes his tail stiff like a cedar; the sinews of his thighs are knit together. His bones are tubes of bronze, his limbs like bars of iron…"
- Science: "Sauropods shared a body plan consisting of: a small head on an extremely long neck; a long, massive body housing an enormous gut; thick pillar-like legs to support the torso; and a very long, tapering, often whiplike tail. A massive hip girdle was fused to the backbone, usually by five sacral vertebrae; this arrangement provided solid support for the body and

tail. The backbone itself was hollowed out at the sides, which thus reduced its weight while retaining structural strength. Sauropods were once thought to have spent their time wallowing in shallow water that would help support their ponderous bodies, but considerable evidence indicates that they were better equipped for living on solid ground."[17]

God also pointed out another feature for Job to consider:

He is the first of the works of God; let him who made him bring near his sword!

This wasn't a statement saying that it was the "first" animal God made. This was a statement about rank and grandeur! God was saying, only the One who made this animal would be big enough and strong enough to judge this enormous beast!

Can one take him by his eyes, or pierce his nose with a snare?

This statement is not just to Job, but to all mankind (which happens to include me and you).

As I've said before, one of the biggest lies we can fall for sometimes is, "You can handle this," "You've got what it takes," or "You've got this under control."

We "handle it." Then when things go wrong, we blame God (or the Devil). It falls right into the current blame culture. "It's somebody else's fault."

We line up all the facts or we have "a strong feeling about this" and when it doesn't go our way, we get upset!

Job was innocent. Even God declared this. What was happening to Job was not because of anything he had done, BUT because of what God was doing!

Job had his defense and the facts on his side. Job would declare his righteousness before God.

God shows Job and us, through those bigger than life situations (our Behemoths) that we can't possibly handle everything.

We can see and understand right from wrong.

We can perceive that we have all the "facts."

We can logically line up all of our arguments!

We can prove our case beyond a shadow of doubt!

BUT we can never stand in the place of God as judge.

Trust in the Lord with all thine heart; and lean not unto thine own understanding. In all thy ways acknowledge Him, and He shall direct thy paths. Be not wise in thine own eyes: fear the Lord, and depart from evil.
— Proverbs 3:5-7 KJV

God has proved Himself trustworthy and righteous. God has demonstrated His wisdom and understanding!

The Lord by wisdom hath founded the earth; by understanding hath he established the heavens. By his knowledge the depth are broken up, and the clouds

> *drop down the dew. My son, let them not depart from thine eyes: keep sound wisdom and discretion…*
>
> — Proverbs 3:19-21

Therefore, we have no place to judge His motives or intentions.

> *"Will you even put me in the wrong? Will you condemn me that you may be in the right? Have you an arm like God, and can you thunder with a voice like his?"*
>
> — Job 40:8-9

Only the One who made you can judge. Only the One who made you can determine the course of your life… "let him who made him bring near his sword!"

I (WE) DON'T HAVE THE QUALIFICATIONS FOR THE JOB!!

---

17 Britannica

CHAPTER 28:
"Can You… Will He… Who Can?" *or* "Your Worst Nightmare!"

As we come to the close of God's discourse with Job, I believe God gets His major point across to Job.

Here in Chapter 41, God describes what is likely the most controversial animal in the entire Bible: Leviathan!

My thoughts and opinions of this terrifying animal are just that — *my* thoughts and opinions.

No one at this time can say exactly what this animal looked like. At this time there is no clear biological or archeological evidence that would adequately show us what this animal was like.

I will state that I am adamant about it not being purely symbolic. I believe God has been pointing out various parts of His Creation. Many of these serve as symbols and representations in various parts of our lives. ALL OF THEM are REAL PHYSICAL OBJECTS and represent His invisible attributes.

Therefore, I see absolutely no reason to switch gears in my interpretation and understanding of God's Words. We cannot dismiss the possible existence of this beast simply because we can't show any physical evidence at this time.

Over and over again, archeological findings prove the accuracy of Scripture. They are finding cities and other artifacts which were previously unknown, except in the Bible.

I hold the same to be true with Creation. I hold to the literal accuracy of the Bible, rather than dismissing it away, because "science says …"

I also hold that there is enough fragmented evidence to put forth a logical defense for the existence of such a beast.

Let's take a look at Leviathan as we listen in on the conversation.

Can you draw out Leviathan with a fishhook or press down his tongue with a cord? Can you put a rope in his nose or pierce his jaw with a hook? Will he make many pleas to you?

Will he speak to you soft words? Will he make a covenant with you to take him for your servant forever?

Will you play with him as with a bird, or will you put him on a leash for your girls?

Will traders bargain over him? Will they divide him up among the merchants?

Can you fill his skin with harpoons or his head with fishing spears?

Lay your hands on him; remember the battle — you will not do it again!

Behold, the hope of a man is false; he is laid low even at the sight of him. No one is so fierce that he dares to stir him up.

Who then is he who can stand before me? Who has first given to me, that I should repay him? Whatever is under the whole heaven is mine.

I will not keep silence concerning his limbs, or his mighty strength, or his goodly frame.

Who can strip off his outer garment?

Who would come near him with a bridle?

Who can open the doors of his face?

Around his teeth is terror. His back is made of rows of shields, shut up closely as with a seal. One is so near to another that no air can come between them.

They are joined one to another; they clasp each other and cannot be separated.

His sneezing flashes forth light, and his eyes are like the eyelids of the dawn. Out of his mouth go flaming torches; sparks of fire leap forth. Out of his nostrils comes forth smoke, as from a boiling pot and burning rushes. His breath kindles coals, and a flame comes forth from his mouth.

In his neck abides strength, and terror dances before him.

The folds of his flesh stick together, firmly cast on him and immovable.

His heart is hard as a stone, hard as the lower millstone.

When he raises himself up, the mighty are afraid; at the crashing they are beside themselves.

Though the sword reaches him, it does not avail, nor the spear, the dart, or the javelin. He counts iron as straw, and bronze as rotten wood. The arrow cannot make him flee; for him, sling stones are turned to stubble. Clubs are counted as stubble; he laughs at the rattle of javelins.

His underparts are like sharp potsherds; he spreads himself like a threshing sledge on the mire. He makes the deep boil like a pot; he makes the sea like a pot of ointment.

Behind him he leaves a shining wake; one would think the deep to be white-haired.

On earth there is not his like, a creature without fear.

> *He sees everything that is high; he is king over all the sons of pride.*
>
> —Job 41:1-34

One does not have to physically experience something in order to know the meaning of a phrase. I could say, "Don't poke a bees' nest!" You may never have done it, but would probably have a pretty good idea of the outcome! If I said, "Don't get between a momma bear and her cubs," again, you may never have even seen a bear, but most people would get the picture.

Here in Job chapter 41, we have an entire chapter (34 verses) devoted to this one animal!

The details boggle the imagination. Leviathan must have been a well-known creature at that time.

The questions God asked Job and the statements of facts leave us with an understanding that Job knew exactly what God was talking about!!

Since no one at this time can give an exact identification of this beast, I can only present the evidence that shows it's possible. The exact identification of this beast was important to Job but doesn't have to be for us, in order to get the message!

Let's look at this through Job's eyes.

While researching this topic, I learned the word *dinosaur* wasn't even around until the mid-1800s. It was introduced into the scientific community by a scientist named Sir Richard Owen. The term *dinosaur* was more narrow, and referred only to reptilian land animals whose hip structures raise them off the ground. Prior to this, the word for a large reptilian beast was *dragon*.

There is a Hebrew word used to describe dragon-like creatures: "tannin" (pronounced 'tan-nene'). This word was used to describe a broad range of reptilians.

There is some confusion here because of two other very similar words (plus the unintended influence of modern science).

- Tanni<u>n</u> is singular and used to designate a creature like a serpent or a dragon.
- Meanwhile the plural form Tanninim as used in Genesis 1:21 is used for "sea creatures."
- Tanni<u>m</u> is the plural form for "jackal."

The Septuagint often translates "tannin" as "drakon" — the Greek word for dragon. If it is correct and proper to distinguish "tannin" (serpent, dragon) from "tannim" (jackal), then we can clearly state that tannin refers to a group of reptiles (either on land or in the sea).

The unfortunate influence of evolutionary thinking has lead many biblical scholars and theologians to discard the possibility that "dragons" ever existed. (For evolutionists, the timeline for creatures such as this creates problems. They claim: "Creatures like the dinosaurs died out 60 million years before humans existed." Therefore, stories of men slaying dragons must be mythical.) Therefore, regrettably some modern Bibles have stopped using the word "dragon" in their translation, due to this evolutionary science.

Accounts of dragons are not always easy to dismiss as mere fantasy. Around the globe and throughout history, in disconnected cultures, the depiction of dragons is undeniable!

Legends, historical accounts, artwork, and the similarities demand a more rational explanation!

- a water monster depicted in an Aboriginal piece,
- an Egyptian historical account of serpents with bat-like wings,
- the poem of Beowulf and a flying fiery serpent (dragon)
- a Native American stone etching that resembles a dragon
- vast amounts of Oriental artwork

The list goes on and on with flags, pottery, and artwork (of all kinds) from around the globe and throughout history.

If the dragon creature is purely mythological, why all the similarities and historical accounts?

I hold that the best explanation of this beast Leviathan comes from the description given in Scripture.

Both Isaiah 27:1 and 51:9 give the impression Leviathan was difficult to kill and states that it was the Lord who slayed the beast.

> *An oracle on the beasts of the Negeb. Through a land of trouble and anguish, from where come the lioness and the lion, the adder and the flying fiery serpent, they carry their riches on the backs of donkey, and their treasures on the humps of camels, to a people that cannot profit them.*
>
> — Isaiah 30:6

If the "flying fiery serpent" is mythical, why don't we take the same approach to the lioness, lion, and adder mentioned in the same passage?

Job 7:12 gives us the idea that it was a powerful and unruly creature that needed to be "watched", "guarded" or "kept in check."

Psalm 104:25-26 says, "Here is the sea, great and wide, which teems with creatures innumerable, living things both small and great. There go the ships, and Leviathan, which You formed to play in it."

In Psalm 104, the Psalmist speaks of God's creation. He presents the sea as expansive and teaming with life. He presents man as traveling these seas (done for commerce and travel) while the Leviathan PLAYS. This creature apparently didn't have a worry and lived without fear of man or predators!

All these historical hints from the Bible refute the idea that the leviathan was a mythical creature that was being used as a literary metaphor. Metaphors don't deflect spears or scare onlookers. In fact, leviathan must have really done these things for God to have actually compared it to His own might.

Identifying the leviathan as a myth only smuggles in the destructive idea that anything in Scripture can be interpreted as a myth or "just symbolic!"

Since the Bible has proven itself true over centuries of scrutiny, I hold to the belief that the leviathan must have really lived. PLUS, God's own mentioning of this beast lends to an understanding that it was real!!!

...On earth there is not his like... No one is so fierce that he dares to stir him up... Who then is he who can stand before me?

Was God comparing Himself to a myth!!?
God did NOT say, "...In man's mind there is not his like..."
Since no modern-day fossil yet exists, any further description, other than that given in Job, would be speculation.

SO, where do we go with this? God has presented Job with a creature that:

- No one can handle — "...*Can you draw out Leviathan with a fishhook or press down his tongue with a cord? Can you put a rope in his nose or pierce his jaw with a hook? ...Who can strip off his outer garment? ...Who would come near him with a bridle? ...Who can open the doors of his face?*"
- Was not friendly — "...*Will he make many pleas to you? Will he speak to you soft words? Will he make a covenant with you to take him for your servant forever? Will you play with him as with a bird, or will you put him on a leash for your girls?...*"
- In fact, Leviathan was terrifying, and if you had the unfortunate experience of tangling with it, you would never forget it and never do it again!!! — "...*Lay your hands on him; remember the battle — you will not do it again! Behold, the hope of a man is false; he is laid low even at the sight of him. No one is so fierce that he dares to stir him up...*"

One could say, "Leviathan was either your 'worst enemy' or worst nightmare!'"

But I don't think God was just trying to scare Job. There was an important point He wanted to make.

CHAPTER 29:

"Do You Realize Who I Am?"

In the final verse of Job 41(vs 34) God's physical description and presentation of Leviathan's nature ends with a very unusual and important statement.

> On earth there is not his like, a creature without fear. He sees everything that is high; he is King over all the sons of pride.

"Without fear" and "Pride"—I can't think of a more deadly combination!

We get a clear picture of who we're dealing with.

These words had to hit Job (as they should us).

(I also think this was a subtle message to Satan as well, since I'm pretty certain that he was on the sidelines watching and listening to all this.)

When all is said and done, going back to the basic foundations is oftentimes the key.

"Without Fear"

> *And to mankind He said, "Behold, the fear of the Lord, that is wisdom; And to turn away from evil is understanding."*
>
> — Job 28:28

> *Furthermore, you shall select out of all the people able men who fear God, men of truth, those who hate dishonest gain; and you shall place these over them as leaders of thousands, of hundreds, of fifties, and of tens.*
>
> — Exodus 18:21

> *You shall stand up in the presence of the grayheaded and honor elders, and you shall fear your God; I am the LORD.*
>
> — Leviticus 19:32

So you shall not wrong one another, but you shall fear your God; for I am the LORD your God.
— Leviticus 25:17

Remember the day you stood before the LORD your God at Horeb, when the LORD said to me, "Assemble the people to Me, that I may have them hear My words so that they may learn to fear Me all the days that they live on the earth, and that they may teach their children."
— Deuteronomy 4:10

"Sons of Pride"

Now I, Nebuchadnezzar, praise, exalt, and honor the King of heaven, for all His works are true and His ways just; and He is able to humble those who walk in pride.
— Daniel 4:37

The fear of the LORD is to hate evil; Pride, arrogance, the evil way, And the perverted mouth, I hate.
— Proverbs 8:13

When pride comes, then comes dishonor; But with the humble there is wisdom.
— Proverbs 11:2

> *Pride goes before destruction, And a haughty spirit before stumbling.*
>
> — Proverbs 16:18

> *And the pride of humanity will be humbled And the arrogance of people will be brought low; And the LORD alone will be exalted on that day.*
>
> — Isaiah 2:17

Are you starting to get the picture?

God has run through all of creation and shown Job the awesomeness of Himself. God has Job now look at himself in order to see who he is, and who he is not! God presents Job with his greatest enemy, an enemy that can destroy him!

- It wasn't the loss of Job's wealth.
- It wasn't the loss of Job's family.
- It wasn't the loss of Job's health.

None of these things destroyed Job!

Not even Leviathan, the dragon, the beast (later to become a symbolic image of Satan.)

Job's real enemy and what he needed to guard himself from was PRIDE! ("WITHOUT FEAR") He was losing his perspective of who God is!!

God knows our hearts, so we might as well be brutally honest with Him. We can tell Him how we feel and what we think. He already knows!! Our thoughts and feelings are not hidden from Him! BUT we can NEVER let ourselves get to the point where we disrespect Him!

> *On earth there is not his like, a creature without fear.*
> *He sees everything that is high…*

Job was very methodical and accurate in defending himself. But Job was now walking the line.

Job's comforters were attacking his character, thus allowing pride an opportunity to crouch at the door.

> *If you do well, will you not be accepted? And if you do not do well, sin is crouching at the door. Its desire is contrary to you, but you must rule over it.*
> — Genesis 4:7 ESV

> *Will you even put me in the wrong? Will you condemn me that you may be in the right?*
> — Job 40:8

We know that pride and boasting is wrong. So we criticize our boss, our spouse or someone else in order to bring them down rather than lifting up ourselves. Dare we even think of doing that with God?!

In Chapter 41, God presents a creature "without equal." Yet, for all its terror, strength, and seemingly invincible attributes, Leviathan was still subject to its Creator.

Job 41:10-11 says, "No one is so fierce that he dares to stir him up. Who then is he who can stand before me? Who has first given to me, that I should repay him? Whatever is under the whole heaven is mine."

God sandwiches this statement in the middle of His description of Leviathan. Thus, in the Hebrew culture, giving it importance.

God doesn't owe Job (or us) an explanation of what He is doing. ("Who has first given to Me that I should repay him?")

He has already demonstrated in creation itself that His ways are far beyond our ability to comprehend (see chapter 11).

It ALL belongs to Him! ("Whatever is under the whole heaven is mine.")

God always seems to bring us back to the beginning!

In God's first encounter with Job (Chapter 38), He brought Job to the beginning of creation. Here in Chapter 41, in God's final discussion with Job, He brings Job all the way back to Job's first discourse. Remember Job Chapter 3? Job sat silent with his friends. He then opened his mouth and spoke, cursing the "day of his birth." (Job's first day!)

All of a sudden, I saw something. I found it strangely funny and profound. I realized as Job mentioned several animals in his lamenting, God used them in His discussion with Job.

The very last animal God presented was the very first animal that Job made reference to:

> Let those curse it who curse the day, Who are prepared to rouse Leviathan.
>
> — Job 3:8

What are your circumstances? That seemingly unconquerable problem? It's out of our control. Things just don't make sense! It's not fair!

Are you under attack? Are you questioning God and His actions, or His apparent lack of action? Where *is* He?

Here, in Leviathan, God shows us our real enemy, an enemy that "plays in the depths" of our day to day lives: "Pride" "without fear"

We can't make friends with it.

We can't make a deal with it.

Our best bet is to try and avoid it all together!

What then is the solution to Job's situation?

We'll see the final outcome in Chapter 42.

CHAPTER 30:

"Get Real!" *or* "Open the Eyes of My Heart, Lord."

Wow! In the past four chapters of the Book of Job, God has taken both Job and us on a walk through His creation.

The question is, *why?*

The Book of Job is classified as wisdom literature. So what are we supposed to glean from this? What can we get from this that we cannot get from watching the National Geographic channel? How can this open our eyes?

Job's final response to God's interaction is what I believe unlocks the answer.

> *Then Job answered the Lord and said: "I know that you can do all things, and that no plan is impossible for you. 'Who is this that hides counsel without knowledge?' Therefore, I have uttered what I did not understand, things too wonderful for me, which I did not know.*
>
> *'Hear and I will speak; I will question you, and you will make it known to me.' I had heard of you by the hearing of the ear, but now my eye sees you; therefore, I despise myself, and repent in dust and ashes."*
>
> — Job 42:1-6

Job has now come full circle:

> *I know that You can do all things, and that no plan is impossible for You.*

Through this tour of creation, Job was brought back to the very beginning of creation itself!

The planning, the foundations, the expanse of the heavens were all displayed! The hidden mysteries of the oceans, light and darkness, even death itself was examined.

Next we saw the animal kingdom. (This was the part of creation that occurred on the same "day" as man.) Here is where God draws the boundaries. He is the One who restrains and provides. Each animal was made by His design and functioned according to His plan. ALL of creation is subject to Him!!

Job could now see and better understand God's omnipotence! But even more, Job acknowledged a better understanding of God's sovereignty and omniscience!!!

...no plan is impossible for you.

Job got a glimpse of the blueprints for creation. They were beyond explanation. Their vastness and intricacies are too great to comprehend completely. Plus, it all works!! Even the ending is planned for!

There is no problem big enough to keep the plan from being completed. (Praise the Lord !)

I personally believe Job did not have a problem with God's sovereignty or His omnipotence. After all, Job feared God.

Many of us know or recognize someone who may have authority over us. Therefore, getting the concept of *sovereignty* is imaginable. Many of us know and recognize someone or something that has power over us. Therefore, getting the concept of *omnipotence* is also imaginable. But none of us know someone who *knows EVERYTHING!* This is probably a harder concept to swallow!

God has a plan, and the workings of it are beyond our understanding! Nevertheless, it works and will be accomplished.

> *'Who is this that hides counsel without knowledge?'*
> *Therefore, I have uttered what I did not understand,*
> *things too wonderful for me, which I did not know.*

I believe God was directing this statement to Job's friends.

> *My wrath is kindled against you and against your*
> *two friends, because you have not spoken of Me what*
> *is trustworthy, as My servant Job has.*
>
> —Job 42:7

But here, Job returns God's quote. In doing this, Job recognized and acknowledged that he (Job) also spoke rashly and out of ignorance.

Job acknowledged, through the vastness of creation, that what he did not know surpassed all that he did know! There were many things just in creation itself beyond his ability to comprehend. How much more his inability to comprehend their Creator.

> *'Hear and I will speak; I will question you, and you*
> *will make it known to me.'*

Job (_____ insert your name here) is now ready to listen. Rather than asserting his right to speak and question one's accuser; Job now asks God for permission to speak!

Rather than demanding an answer from God and have Him give an account of Himself, Job acknowledged, "God has not been silent!"

Job never received an explanation as to what was going on. That piece of information no longer mattered.

The prosecutor/judge vs defendant scenario was over!

Job had faced his Leviathan (pride) and replaced it with humility. (This is a whole new topic.)

Now comes the statement that has followed me from my early days as a young Christian. I was looking for answers to the changes that were taking place in my life. From the day I first read it, the Holy Spirit told me, "Here is your answer." (Thus the title of this book.)

> *I had heard of you by the hearing of the ear, but now my eye sees you.*

Wow!

Let me make one thing VERY CLEAR. We are not talking pantheism here! Nature is NOT GOD! We don't have to appease the spirit of a tree or thank a deer for sacrificing itself so I can eat.

This is in direct conflict with what is going on:

> *For since the creation of the world God's invisible qualities — his eternal power and divine nature — have been clearly seen, being understood from what has been made, so that people are without excuse. For even though they knew God, they did not honor Him as God or give thanks, but they became futile in their reasonings, and their senseless hearts were darkened. Claiming to be wise, they became fools, and they exchanged the glory of the incorruptible God for an*

> *image in the form of corruptible mankind, of birds, four-footed animals, and crawling creatures.*
>
> — Romans 1:20-23

When we look at nature, we are not seeing God. What we are seeing is God *expressing* Himself. He is putting forth a physical example of an invisible quality.

We do this ourselves, as we try to teach or learn a new concept.

In kindergarten you learned 2+2=4. How?

Probably by examples, like:

🍎🍎 + 🍎🍎 = 🍎🍎🍎🍎

We put a tangible example to an invisible concept. As adults, architects and engineers often build three-dimensional models in order to visualize the plans that they have. The list of examples is almost endless.

God has done that in creation for us!

> *...therefore, I despise myself, and repent in dust and ashes.*

As any good Bible teacher would say, "What is the 'therefore' there for?" Job just walked through a very detailed physical series of examples of God's invisible qualities. He looks around himself in the midst of this storm and says, "I see You, Lord!" Therefore, Job is settled back into the place of being God's humble servant. The fear of God (recognizing who He is in relation to who we are). The beginning of wisdom. Job went back to the beginning.

When Job said "I despise myself" this was not saying that he hated himself. He was actually retracting, taking an eraser to those things that he had said in the previous chapters.

> *The Hebrew word literally means, from the standpoint of etymology, to disappear; from the standpoint of usage, to retract, to repudiate. As a matter of fact, Job at this point went beyond what he had previously said when he declared, 'I am of small account' and declared that he practically cancelled himself entirely. I disappear, I retract all that has been said; I repudiate the position I have taken up.*
> — Reverend Doctor George Campbell Morgan D.D., a British evangelist, preacher, a leading Bible teacher, and a prolific author

While much of what Job said was true.

> *After the Lord had said these things to Job, he said to Eliphaz the Temanite, "I am angry with you and your two friends, because you have not spoken the truth about me, as my servant Job has."*
> — Job 42:7

Job recognized he had spoken out of place. He erred when he cursed the day he was born. He erred when he despaired of his condition and challenged God in doing so! He erred when he questioned the benefits of living a good life and the resulting life hereafter.

The standards for sin have not changed ... "whatever is not from faith is sin" (Romans 14:23).

Job at times had questioned God's actions. (Many of us have done that in the course of our walk with the Lord.) Yet! Even with all this complaining and questioning, Job did NOT curse God, which had been Satan's goal (Job 1:11, 2:5)! Therefore, God wins!!

Job saw that he spoke from a position of ignorance and a lack of understanding. Only God truly sees the big picture!

Job now returns to his previous humble state (a normal response when presented with the presence of God.) He realized that even with his vast understanding of God, along with his close relationship and love for Him, the amount that he did not know was greater than what he did know.

Seeing God's creation through fresh eyes gave Job what he needed.

- Job was able to see God's omnipotence.
- Job was able to see God's omniscience and that He has a plan.
- Job was able to see that even those things that don't make sense happen "by His purpose" and function exactly as He desires.
- Job was able to see that God sets the boundaries and by His provision everything is sustained.
- Job was able to see God's omnipresence, and understood that He was with him in his crisis!!
  — God is in control!!

This AWESOME presence of God humbled Job!!

And he said to man, "Behold, the fear of the Lord, that is wisdom, and to turn away from evil is understanding."

— Job 28:28 ESV

THIS is an important lesson — JOB BECAME CONTENT IN NOT KNOWING WHY!

Standing in the presence of God, Job had every opportunity to ask, "WHY?" But he didn't, because it was no longer important!

CHAPTER 31:

"Why?"

Don't get me wrong. Over the years that I've had the privilege and blessings of walking with God, I <u>still</u> often ask "why?"

Hopefully, I've learned to realize God is under no obligation to answer. I also realize that even if He did answer — I may not understand the reason or reasons for something.

Revelation can be defined as "the bringing to light something that was previously obscure or completely hidden or to uncover."

When it comes to understanding what God has for us, we often refer to two kinds of revelation.

The first is general or natural revelation.

The second is called specific or special revelation.

In the past few chapters of Job, we've received a quick overview and journey through a small portion of God's natural revelation.

This is God uncovering and shining a light on His very existence. He reveals His nature and His position as He relates to all of creation.

This is the revelation that is available to ALL mankind. This is the revelation that Paul writes of in Romans:

> *For what can be known about God is plain to them, because God has shown it to them. For his invisible attributes, namely, His eternal power and divine nature, have been clearly perceived, ever since the creation of the world, in the things that have been made. So they are without excuse. For although they knew God, they did not honor Him as God or give thanks to Him, but they became futile in their*

thinking, and their foolish hearts were darkened. Claiming to be wise, they became fools, and exchanged the glory of the immortal God for images resembling mortal man and birds and animals and creeping things.

— Romans 1:19-23

This is not God's complete revelation, but it is the primary revelation that "cannot be ignored." There is ONE God and ONE Creator.

Overlooking God's revelation through nature is taking His work (including us) lightly. Satan loves it when we don't give recognition to God's handiwork or try to explain it away through science.

Yet, true science does ask the question, "Why?" I would best define science as "The pursuit and application of knowledge and understanding pertaining to the natural and social world, by both subjective and objective data." Any good scientist knows there must be a way to look at the data objectively and subjectively. Without both types of data, it can be hard to have a full picture and understanding of what is being studied.

By definition, subjective data is collected or obtained via personal interactions, i.e., talking, sharing, explaining, etc. Subjective data is collected to make an assumption about what the fact might be, what event might have occurred, or what calculations may have to be done, etc..

- Subjective data can also be collected by means of judgment, suspicion, or rumors.

- This data can vary from one person to another, with every situation and minute.
- It cannot be declared as the truth, as it evolves from so many varied sources with different inputs.
- Subjective language often begins with, "I think," "I need," or "I feel." Subjective language often contains the words "possible" or "may."

On the other hand, by definition objective data is factual information collected through direct observation or measurement.

- Objective data is true regardless and does not vary from one person, situation, or time to another. Objective data is true regardless of the feelings or opinions of the person presenting or receiving the information.
- Objective data will be the same from multiple sources and can be counted, described, and confirmed accurately. Objective data does not vary from one person to another nor with various situations.

Many of the problems today come when scientists mix subjective data with objective data, thereby presenting both as fact! (Remember, subjective data cannot be declared as the truth, as it evolves from so many varied sources with different inputs.)

We don't always catch those quickly spoken and very subtle words: "Think, could, possible, believe, etc...." If we listened closely, we would realize in some cases a vast amount of "facts" being taught are nothing more than speculative possibilities and opinions (based on subjective data).

There are times when "ideas" taught as "fact" are truly based upon "other ideas." (Subjective date based on subjective data.) This can go on and on until the "objective data" either no longer is present or is even contradicted altogether!

In this exploration of creation and "objective data," God reveals Himself to all of mankind. All being said, God's general or natural revelation can and should be explored by science. True science asks the questions "Why?" and "How?"

A deeper understanding and appreciation for creation can and should lead us to a deeper and greater appreciation for our God. We too can have our eyes opened.

> *For in him all things were created: things in heaven and on earth, visible and invisible, whether thrones or powers or rulers or authorities; all things have been created through him and for him. He is before all things, and in him all things hold together.*
> — Colossians 1:16-17

I hold that this above statement is true for creation in totality! It not only explains such facts as the strong nuclear force or other forces that hold atoms together, but the entire universe as well. God is the reason for both forces that are seen in the expanding and contracting views of the universe.

For behold, I create new heavens and a new earth; and the former shall not be remembered or come to mind. But be glad and rejoice forever in what I create; for behold, I create a Jerusalem as a rejoicing, and her people a joy.

— Isaiah 65:17-19

Of old, You laid the foundation of the earth, and the heavens are the work of Your hands. They will perish, but You will endure; yes, all of them will grow old like a garment, like a cloak You will change them, and they will be changed. But You are the same, and Your years will have no end.

— Psalm 102:25-27

Looking for and hastening the coming of the day of God, because of which the heavens will be dissolved being on fire, and the elements will melt with fervent heat… Nevertheless we, according to His promise, look for a new heaven and a new earth in which righteousness dwells.

— 2 Peter 3:12-13

Then I saw a new heaven and a new earth, for the first heaven and the first earth had passed away, and the sea was no more.

— Revelation 21:1

When God says "new" that's exactly what He means. It's not going to be a repair or restoration of what we currently know. He's just going to let go and make new. And, unlike this present creation He's not going to take seven days to do it!!

When we hear the statement, "You can't 'prove' the existence of God!" our response should be: "To the contrary, He has already proven Himself. What cannot be 'proven' that He does not exist."

So, how does all this "general or natural revelation" found in the Book of Job solve Job's problem? (Better yet, how does it give *us* an answer to *our* problems?)

I believe our difficulty comes from trying to solve life's problems with science! Physical science was not meant to answer the "whys" and "how comes" of our personal lives! How can I say that?

- If my above statement is true, "Why does God respond to Job's question of 'why?' by giving him a crash course in creation?!"
- If my above statement is true, "Why was Job satisfied with God's response?" God never answered the question!
- If my above statement is true, "What are we to learn from the Book of Job and creation in our dealings with our questions of WHY to life's problems?"
- If my above statement is true, "Why am I even bothering to write this book?"

The answer is simple. (See answer in next chapter.)

CHAPTER 32:

Not "Why?" but "Who?"

To be honest, there are times when God wants us to ask "Why?"

In the same way that we research and dig deeper in order to understand something about His creation (God wants us to "walk in the recesses of the deep" and discover that which can only be "found by searching," as discussed in Job 38:16 and Chapter 10 of this book), God wants us to "dig deeper" into His Word and seek His face.

Often when people finish reading the Book of Job, they are left with the same question as the title of a popular book, why do bad things happen to…

Or, when we're going through a trial (and sometimes feeling sorry for ourselves) we speak of relating to Job and his suffering. We try to come up with that ever elusive answer — WHY is this happening to me?

I'm not saying God never answers that question.

There <u>are</u> many times when we need to know why. Sometimes God wants to redirect us, move us forward, or even discipline us for something and make us stop.

But what are we to do with those vast number of times when God seems to remain silent on this issue?

May I suggest a possible reason?

The answer to the statement is simple: we're asking the wrong question!

Think for a moment.

Job's friends were trying to say Job's sin or secret disobedience was the reason or cause for his suffering (the why!). This in turn had Job questioning God's reason for doing things (the why!).

We have an insight that Job didn't have (God's conversation with Satan). The reason for Job's troubles (the why) was plain and simple: Satan's desire to rebel against God, and God's response to Satan's accusations against Him.

But where does that leave Job (and us)?

If we don't ask the *right question* and don't approach our lives and trials from a *proper perspective,* we can end up in a world of hurt!

There are those who hold a view of God called deism. Deism believes that a personal god created the world, set it in motion, but then backed off! The god of deism does not play an active role in His world, but allows the universe to run by natural and self-sustaining laws that He established. Although the deists believe in a supernatural creation of the world, they do not believe in supernatural intervention in the world.

Both deism and a "scientific" look at creation leave us with a lot of questions:

- Why am I here?
- What is the purpose of my life?
- Am I nothing more than a mass of cells?
- Why is there evil in the world?
- What happens to me after I die?

Science and deism don't answer those questions.

Biblical Christianity answers ALL these questions and more through the Scriptures and the person of Jesus Christ.

You see, God doesn't just want us to know that He exists. God wants us to know Him and have a relationship with Him.

This is where specific or special revelation comes into play. This specific or special revelation comes in the form of His direct communication. This appears many times in the Old Testament or in the New Testament as with Saul on the road to Damascus and other times. It comes in the form of the Word (the inspired Scriptures or Bible). Lastly it comes in the person of Jesus Christ. (Hebrews 1:3, "The Son is the radiance of God's glory and the exact representation of his being ....")

It's in this personal relationship that we find both the right questions and often the right answers.

Throughout God's entire discourse with Job, God's focus was on <u>who</u>: "Look at Me, Job. Forget trying to figure out why."

> *"For my thoughts are not your thoughts, neither are your ways my ways," declares the Lord. "As the heavens are higher than the earth, so are my ways higher than your ways and my thoughts than your thoughts."*
>
> — Isaiah 55:8-9

God says, "Look around you and remember WHO I AM!!"

We can study a work of art.

We can admire the handiwork of a craftsman.

We can read great writings and study brilliant thinkers.

We can know A LOT ABOUT the artist, craftsman, writer, and thinker, all without ever KNOWING them!! All without it being PERSONAL!!

It is in this personal specific/special revelation of Himself and His purposeful interaction with us that Job found his answer (and where we also are to find ours).

It is through this special/specific revelation that we get a clear picture of WHO God is. We get a picture of WHO we are and what God has and wants for us.

Job (as most of us), in the midst of his suffering and the accusations of his friends, turned his focus *off* the God he knew. Job was *now* looking at his situation and relying on his own understanding. Job had started asking the wrong question: "WHY?" not "WHO?" Job needed to revisit who God IS.

At the beginning of his trials, Job's focus was on God.

> *Then Job got up, tore his robe, and shaved his head; then he fell to the ground and worshiped. And he said, "Naked I came from my mother's womb, and naked shall I return. The Lord gave and the Lord has taken away; blessed be the name of the Lord." In all this Job did not sin or charge God with wrong.*
>
> —Job 1:20-22

> *But he said to her, "You speak as one of the foolish women would speak. Shall we receive good from God, and shall we not receive evil?" In all this Job did not sin with his lips.*
>
> —Job 2:10

Job wasn't asking "Why?" Job acknowledged WHO was in control. We would be wise to follow the same.

In Chapter 3, Job was in what I would consider a pretty deep state of depression. He was probably thinking the life he knew was over and he was going to die destitute and suffering. This is when Job started asking the "Why?" Still believing all he knew about God, Job just couldn't wrap his head around what God was doing. (Why?)

Job knew that he was heading down a dead end road. But in his defense against his "friends'" accusations, he had no answer. (Read Job 9.)

Then in chapter 19, in one of those up and down moments, Job declared what I think is one of the most powerful statements in the Bible.

> *For I know that my Redeemer lives, and at the last he will stand upon the earth. And after my skin has been thus destroyed, yet in my flesh I shall see God, whom I shall see for myself, and my eyes shall behold, and not another. My heart faints within me!*
>
> — Job 19:25-27

Job looked at the "WHO"... His "Redeemer"... His "goel."

> *The "Goel" stood for another to defend his cause, to avenge wrongs done to him, and so to acquit him of all charges laid against him.*
>
> — G. Campbell Morgan

> *A redeemer was a vindicator of one unjustly wronged. He was a defender of the oppressed. A champion of the suffering. An advocate of one unjustly accused. If you were ever wronged, a redeemer would come and stand beside you as your champion and advocate.*
>
> — Steven J. Lawson,
> Lead Preacher of Trinity Bible Church of Dallas, founder and president of OnePassion Ministries

> *The word is important in Old Testament jurisprudence. It had both a criminal and a civil aspect. As blood avenger, a goel had a responsibility to avenge*

> *the blood of a slain kinsman (Numbers 35:12-28). He was not seeking revenge but justice. On the civil side he was a redeemer or vindicator. Here he had the responsibility to buy back and so redeem the lost inheritance of a deceased relative... As such, he was the defender or champion of the oppressed.*
>
> — Elmer Bernard Smick,
> Old Testament scholar, professor, and former president of the Evangelical Theological Society

Job's (our) Redeemer was not just a wishful idea.

Job's (our) Redeemer was not philosophical.

Job's (our) Redeemer is "REAL" (… he will stand upon the earth).

Job's situation didn't fit into the current theological understanding of God. Everyone knows bad things happen to bad people.

Job's "friends" continued to paint him in a bad light and pushed the concept that God was acting as a righteous JUDGE. Satan's game plan was the same in the beginning, presenting half truths and falsely speaking of "God's motives." (Genesis 3:1-5)

God was going to use His perceived silence about the reason for Job's situation to teach more about Himself and correct that misplaced understanding.

The WHO is more important than the why!

CHAPTER 33:

"It's Not What You Know but Who You Know" *or* "It's Not WHAT You See but WHO You See!"

I have heard of You by the hearing of the ear, But now my eye sees You. Therefore I abhor myself, and repent in dust and ashes.

— Job 42:5-6

For since the creation of the world His invisible attributes are clearly seen, being understood by the things that are made, even His eternal power and Godhead, so that they are without excuse.

— Romans 1: 20

In my house, I have the privilege of owning several paintings done by my younger brother, Bruce. He has his studio not far from me. I've had the opportunity to see some of his work start from an empty canvas and transform into a thing of beauty. I get to hear the story about the painting, why he's doing it and sometimes even where it's going.

Even though the paintings that I have are things of beauty and have great financial value if I were to sell them (an unthinkable act that will never happen) that is NOT the source of their worth. All these paintings are priceless works of art not only because of who the artist is, but because of my relationship with the artist!

All of creation points us to God! All of creation is meant to glorify God! It's not what we see but WHO, and our response to that experience is what makes the difference.

Coming to a better understanding of who God is and what He is like is essential to one's faith. Scripture tells us, "His invisible attributes…. His eternal power and Godhead" are clearly seen and understood through creation.

Job had a personal relationship with God. Job understood God's promise of redemption (Job 19:25). What God did in His discourse with Job was to strengthen that bond.

I can hear God saying, "Job, look at all of creation and see Me. I made all this and I made you. All creation is subject to Me as are you. I sustain all creation as I sustain you. I care for all creation, and I care for you. I am here, Job, just look around you and see what I've done. I'm here, Job, just look around and see what I am doing. I'm here, Job, just look around and see that I've got everything under control. I'm here, Job, look around and see Me.

"See, understand, and believe that what I plan to do and all that I promised will happen. Your Redeemer lives."

Job could "see" that God had a plan. He could "see" that God was in complete control. Job could "see" there were parts of God's plan he could neither see nor understand. But Job could not see the whole picture. How could he? God has not finished it yet!

For us today, God gets a little more specific. The Bible and the life of Jesus Christ reveal God's character in a way that creation itself cannot. God makes it personal.

Jesus Christ is God's full expression of His character.

> *God, who at various times and in various ways spoke in time past to the fathers by the prophets, has in these last days spoken to us by His Son, whom He has appointed heir of all things, through whom also He made the worlds; who being the brightness of His glory and the express image of His person, and upholding all things by the word of His power, when He had by Himself purged our sins, sat down at the right hand of the Majesty on high, having become so much better than the angels, as He has by inheritance obtained a more excellent name than they.*
>
> — Hebrews 1:1-4

Jesus Christ expressed the full person of God. Christ exemplified those transmutable qualities of God's character: God's love, justice, patience, gentleness, compassion, and integrity. These were all lived out in the life of Jesus Christ.

> *Jesus said to him, "Have I been with you so long, and yet you have not known Me, Philip? He who has seen Me has seen the Father; so how can you say, 'Show us the Father?' Do you not believe that I am in the Father, and the Father in Me? The words that I speak*

to you I do not speak on My own authority; but the Father who dwells in Me does the works. Believe Me that I am in the Father and the Father in Me, or else believe Me for the sake of the works themselves."
— John 14:9-11

But without faith it is impossible to please Him, for he who comes to God must believe that He is, and that He is a rewarder of those who diligently seek Him.
— Hebrews 11:6

Jesus said to him, "I am the way, the truth, and the life. No one comes to the Father except through Me."
— John 14:6 (NKJV)

He is the image of the invisible God, the firstborn of all creation. For by Him all things were created, in heaven and on earth, visible and invisible, whether thrones or dominions or rulers or authorities – all things were created through him and for him. And He is before all things and in him all things hold together. And He is the head of the body, the church. He is the beginning, the first born of the dead, that in everything He might have preeminence. For in Him the fullness of God was pleased to dwell, and through Him to reconcile to Himself all things, whether on earth or in heaven, making peace by the blood of His cross.
— Colossians 1: 15-20

All of creation points to God. All of creation was created through Jesus Christ. All of creation was for Jesus Christ. Jesus Christ is the image of the invisible God.

I understand that currently we live in a society and culture that has turned its back on God. It promotes the idea that anyone who holds to Creation and a Creator is blind to science and is holding on to nothing more than a religious belief. Some have gone so far as to call it a myth and claim it to be on the same level as Greek mythology.

It is at this point that we come to a whole new discussion, which would require a whole new book to examine the truth. My point here is not to scientifically prove the existence of God. That's not my responsibility. I hold on to the view that the One True God has already proven Himself. He has already stated that He has done that clearly. I believe it would be arrogant on my part to think I could do a better job!

Instead, I hope to simply see.

Instead, I hope to encourage others to simply see.

So that at the end of the day we can say, "I had heard of You by the hearing of the ear, but now my eye sees you; therefore, I despise myself, and repent in dust and ashes" (Job 42:5-6)

AFTERWORD

I've now been walking with the Lord for almost 50 years. I make no claim of being a great theologian, scientist, or author. Any information shared in this book is the product of many great men and women who have "walked in the recesses of the deep" and "observed that which is only found by searching."

I've collected and put together the information in this book as much for my benefit as for those who read it. I do not hold to these truths with any hope of winning a debate on the existence of God. That is not the purpose of this book. I do not hold to these truths with any hope of explaining why God does what He does. That is not the purpose of this book.

The purpose of this book is to express to both myself and the reader the foundational and important truths that can be seen in what biblical scholars call general revelation.

I believe that from all the truths and wisdom found in the Book of Job, two of the most important lessons are humility and an awestruck respect of who God is.

> *The Lord said to Satan, "Have you considered My servant Job? For there is no One like him on earth, a blameless and upright man, fearing God and turning away from evil."*
>
> *Then Satan answered the Lord, "Does Job fear God for nothing?"*
>
> — Job 1:8-9

For the despairing man there should be kindness from his friend; So that he does not abandon the fear of the Almighty.

— Job 6:14

And to mankind He said, "Behold, the fear of the Lord, that is wisdom; And to turn away from evil is understanding."

— Job 28:28

Listen to this, Job; Stand and consider the wonders of God. Do you know how God establishes them, and makes the lightning of His clouds to shine? Do you know about the hovering of the clouds, the wonders of the One who is perfect in knowledge, you whose garments are hot when the land is still because of the south wind? Can you, with Him, spread out the skies, strong as a cast metal mirror? Teach us what we are to say to Him; we cannot present our case because of darkness. Shall it be told Him that I would speak? Or should a man say that he would be swallowed up? Now people do not see the light which is bright in the skies; but the wind has passed and cleared them. From the north comes golden splendor; around God is awesome majesty. The Almighty - we cannot find Him; He is exalted in power and He will not violate justice and abundant righteousness. Therefore people fear Him; He does not regard any who are wise of heart.

— Job 37:14-24

As Christians, we don't have the right to exploit nature (a position opposite that expressed by Lynn White in his book *The Historical Roots of Present Day Ecological Crisis*, 1967). Instead, we are obligated by our relationship with the Creator to be good stewards of His creation, to cultivate it and keep it.

> *And the Lord God took the man and put him in the garden of Eden to do work in it and take care of it.*
> — Genesis 2:15 (BBE)

My prayer is that you come to a closer relationship with God through Jesus Christ.